GOVERNING
ON THE
GROUND

**THE PAST, PRESENT, AND FUTURE
OF COUNTY GOVERNMENT**

PETER GOLDEN

ARCHWAY
PUBLISHING

Archway Publishing books may be ordered through booksellers or by contacting:

Archway Publishing
1663 Liberty Drive
Bloomington, IN 47403
www.archwaypublishing.com
844-669-3957

Cover design by Leon Lawrence III

All photos published with permission.

ISBN: 978-1-6657-3636-7 (sc)
ISBN: 978-1-6657-3637-4 (hc)
ISBN: 978-1-6657-3638-1 (e)

Library of Congress Control Number: 2023900102

Print information available on the last page.

Archway Publishing rev. date: 01/16/2023

This book is dedicated to America's 3.6 million county employees and nearly 40,000 county elected officials, who selflessly serve our residents and communities. Their commitment to public service and problem-solving is indispensable.

TABLE OF CONTENTS

Health

Human Services

Public Safety

The Environment and Land Use

Community and Economics

Transportation

Technology

FOREWORD

By National Association of Counties CEO/
Executive Director Matthew Chase

America's 40,000 elected county officials and 3.6 million county employees are heirs of the past, guardians of the present and, with careful planning and vision, creators of a better future.

As you will read in these pages, control of local affairs is an American obsession dating to 1620 when the passengers on The Mayflower signed their compact and became the first people in Western history to form a government of individuals without the oversight of a king or queen.

Fourteen years later, the first county was formed in Virginia, and over the next four centuries, counties grew, merged, changed names, and were defined—and redefined—by geographical boundaries. Currently, half of Americans live in large urban counties while the remaining half reside in counties that are primarily rural, suburban, or a mix.

Counties provide services ranging from transportation to infrastructure, from health to justice to public safety, to almost any assistance you can imagine. NACo was founded nearly ninety years ago, yet our mission, as clearly articulated by our elected leaders, remains the same—to strengthen America's counties as communities and public institutions, ultimately helping people and places to thrive. We pursue this vision by harnessing the collective power, knowledge, and innovations of county officials.

With a shared focus on promoting healthy, safe, and vibrant counties, as originally outlined by our nation's founders through the concepts of "ordered liberty" and "federalism," NACo and our county officials are essential players in our intergovernmental system of federal, state, local, and tribal governments, a complex, often misunderstood structure charged with the sharing and balance of power and responsibilities among levels of government.

Serving our nation's county officials is a labor of love and has taught me that I am still, at my core, the boy who grew up surrounded by the mountains, lakes, and farmland of Washington County in upstate New York. In fact, it was during the bright seasons of my adolescence, seeing how small-town people were invariably willing to lend each other a hand, and living with a stepfather who served as the district attorney and then a judge, that I discovered the power and efficacy of county government—the satisfactions of solving local challenges and supporting those in need.

One regrettable—and inaccurate—perception of county government is that it's an anonymous, unfeeling bureaucracy that people think of as "They." In reality, it is "We," because the individuals filling these roles are our neighbors, friends, and family. Seeking to showcase the humanity and drive of these public servants, this book highlights how thirty county officials faced challenges in the past and try to anticipate how they will face new challenges in the future. You will learn, through personal anecdotes and a behind-the-scenes look at their work, just how resourceful and impactful local government leaders can be.

I admire their creativity, and I am in awe of their courage. Frankly, public officials operate at a disadvantage compared to private-sector leaders. In the private sector, innovation is celebrated and rewarded. Tragically, in the public sector, innovation is too often investigated and castigated. A news headline asks, "Why are they doing that?" and implies that something unethical or, even worse, illegal is underway. This is a death blow to innovation and explains why our elected leaders are becoming increasingly risk-averse, and it is this aversion that allows problems to fester and expand, contributing to society's decline.

However, as you will read in these thirty remarkable stories, confronting the unprecedented challenges of the recent past—a global pandemic, economic uncertainty, deadly and destructive natural disasters, and civil unrest—county officials held steady and focused on balancing public health, safety, and economic security, regardless of the public scrutiny and drubbing that naturally follows. And I am convinced that in the coming years communities will increasingly rely on county government. Here's why.

Even as our economy becomes more intertwined globally, people and goods are freer to move around the world and more media attention is fixated on national politics and personalities. Even so, our daily lives—the foundation of our Republic—depend on decisions carried out at the local level.

County leaders are on the front lines. When a road needs repaving, a family member overdoses from a fentanyl-laced substance, or nursing-home patients are overwhelmed by COVID-19, residents expect results. They care about their pot-holed ruined tires or whether their loved ones will survive the virus. End of story. No debate about it.

Democracies are messy. Fragile. Even frustratingly slow. Yet as our Founding Fathers laid out during the uncertain years of the American Revolution, our form of government is worth fighting to protect. Luckily, county officials continue to safeguard and advance our quality of life, from our elections, to public safety and emergency services, to community assets and infrastructure.

Counties have long been the building blocks of our nation. For too long, our county officials have worked in the background. Now, at last, with this book, they are stepping out into the spotlight.

BY THE PEOPLE, FOR THE PEOPLE

Counties: The Building Blocks of America

In essence, county government began on a cold November day in 1620 as The Mayflower dropped anchor off the coast of Cape Cod. The thirty-five-man crew[1] and 102 passengers were anxious to go ashore after sailing across a testy sea for two months.[2] The problem was rooted in the fact that only about one-third of the passengers were Pilgrims, members of a radical Puritan sect that wanted to separate from the Church of England. Most of the passengers—called "strangers" by the Pilgrims—were laborers, artisans, indentured servants, a soldier, a sexton, and a former assistant to an ambassador. And now, as the passenger William Bradford would record in his journal, the strangers let loose with "mutinous speeches," saying that once on land "they would use their liberty" and no one would have the "power to command them."[3]

The strangers' rebelliousness endangered the potential community, and the solution was to draw up an agreement. Later referred to as the Mayflower Compact, the agreement stated that the passengers would join in *"a Civil Body Politic .... [and] enact, constitute and frame such just and equal Laws, Ordinances, Acts, Constitutions and Offices .... for the general good of the Colony, unto which we promise all due submission and obedience."*[4]

The Pilgrims and strangers were not the first colonists in the New World. In 1607, a colony had been established in Jamestown, Virginia. It was a business venture undertaken by the Virginia Company of London with the permission of King James I, and from its founding comes the origin of counties in the New World. In 1619, the Virginia Company established four "citties"—with the names James, Charles, Elizabeth, and Henrico. Fifteen years later, a new king, Charles I, would create eight shires in Virginia, the Anglo-Saxon version of counties. James

Cittie would turn into James City Shire, and by the end of the next decade, the name was James City County. The first legislative assembly met in Jamestown in 1619. The English king retained the power to rule the colonies, but the colonists, claiming their rights as English citizens, chose to elect their own representatives.[5]

This government was different than the one agreed to by the passengers on the Mayflower because their compact, as historian Rebecca Fraser notes, was "the first experiment in consensual government in Western history between individuals with one another, and not with a monarch."[6]

Yet, equally important, is the reason behind the legislative assembly and the compact, for both highlight a facet of the American character. We began as a nation of immigrants. By definition, immigrants are not satisfied with their present situation. (Native Americans and African slaves were not immigrants, and their dissatisfaction with their lot would understandably surpass that of the new arrivals.) Whether fleeing poverty or seeking freedom from a repressive regime, the immigrant's instinct is to create a better life, frequently at great personal risk.

Americans have preserved that spirit. They dislike overlords meddling in their lives, which, in the aftermath of the Revolutionary War, presented a challenge to the Founders who faced constructing a government for people inclined to resent government.

That resentment boiled over in the summer of 1786 when farmers in Massachusetts—crushed by debt and infuriated by taxes—launched a violent revolt. Named for one its leaders, Daniel Shays, the violence continued until the state recruited a private militia that put an end to it in the winter of 1787.

Three months later, the Constitutional Convention was called to order in Philadelphia. In the disquieting shadow of Shays' Rebellion, many of the delegates pressed for a far stronger central government. These Federalists—led by Alexander Hamilton—found themselves in conflict with the Anti-Federalists, whose most famous spokesman would be Thomas Jefferson. During the convention, Jefferson was serving as a minister to France. However, Elbridge Gerry of Massachusetts was in Philadelphia. He refused to sign the Constitution and outlined his objections in an essay, writing that the powers of the national government were "indefinite and dangerous," and the document lacked "the security of a bill of rights" for states and citizens.[7] His essay was so popular it went through forty-six printings.[8]

The Constitution was ratified on June 22, 1788, after nine of the thirteen state legislatures voted in favor of it, but the call for more enumerated rights persisted. The holdout states dropped their objections by the end of 1791, after ten amendments, known as the Bill of Rights, were added to the Constitution—beginning with freedom of religion, speech, the press, and the right of assembly; and concluding with an amendment that would be crucial to the growth of local government: *The powers not delegated to the United States by the Constitution, nor prohibited by it to the states, are reserved to the states respectively, or to the people.*[9]

Almost immediately, the new central government was tested. Secretary of the Treasury Alexander Hamilton wanted to levy a tax on domestically produced spirits. After Congress approved the tax, farmers and distillers in Western Pennsylvania objected to it. When their objections included burning the home of a tax collector, President George Washington led over twelve thousand militiamen out west, and the Whiskey Rebellion was finished. In 1802, President Thomas Jefferson, his antipathy to Hamilton's Federalism undiminished, did away with the tax.[10]

Even though the United States nearly doubled in size when Jefferson completed the Louisiana Purchase in 1803, Americans' desire to control local affairs was still intact in 1831 when the Frenchman Alexis de Tocqueville arrived in Newport, Rhode Island, and began traveling the country, taking notes and conducting interviews that he would use to write the classic, *Democracy in America.*

Tocqueville was impressed by "the spectacle of a society of going forward all by itself," which was so unlike monarchal France, where decisions were determined by the central government in Paris and hindered progress in the towns and villages.[11] The freedom to shape your own community, Tocqueville believed, suited the "enterprising, adventurous, and above all, [innovative Americans]."[12]

***

During the middle years of the twentieth century, civil rights advocates sought relief from the Supreme Court, the president, and Congress. By then, decision-makers in Washington, D.C., had gradually reduced the local control of citizens' lives—so much so that by the twenty-first century, a Gallup Poll revealed that 59 percent of Americans believed the federal government was too powerful.[13]

How did this happen? Unquestionably, the Civil War and the fight for civil rights contributed to it. As did the fact that the country became more complicated to manage as the population jumped from 34 million in 1860[14] to 179 million in 1960,[15] and people poured out of small farming communities to work at factories in the cities where elected officials were more likely to be seen in newspapers than on doorsteps.[16]

In response to the Great Depression, President Franklin Delano Roosevelt's New Deal programs significantly expanded the role of the federal government. Even as memories of the Great Depression faded, Americans wanted the New Deal programs maintained and increasingly turned to Washington, D.C., for help with projects that, prior to FDR, had chiefly been the responsibility of local government[17]—the construction of low-income housing and highways [18] and funding for public schools.[19]

***

In an era of accelerating federalism that would have stunned Alexander Hamilton, it would be understandable if county government disappeared in the blizzard of national programs. Yet county officials had long been the forgotten men and women of government. In 1917, Henry Stimson Gilbertson published a study of counties, referring to them as "the dark continent of American politics," and stating that the "average

American" believed county government was "a headless institution where responsibility is scattered in a thousand different directions."[20]

This was an inaccurate characterization. County commissioners, clerks, sheriffs, and justices of the peace were generally known in their communities. The perception of them as "scattered" was the consequence of their legal status as mere administrative vassals of the state. Their status started to change in the nineteenth century. "Home rule" charters were enacted by some state legislatures, granting counties a measure of autonomy.[21] This led to a power struggle between counties and states that was reminiscent of the struggle between Federalists and Anti-Federalists, and in short order it wound up in the courts.

In 1868, home rule suffered a defeat when Judge John F. Dillon of the Iowa Supreme Court ruled that counties "derive their powers and rights wholly from [the state] legislature."[22] The "Dillon Rule" was not the final word. In 1871, a Michigan Supreme Court case led to an opinion from a distinguished constitutional scholar, Judge Thomas M. Cooley, who determined that "local government is [a] matter of absolute right; and the state cannot take it away."[23] In 1907, Cooley's opinion was opposed when the United States Supreme Court sided with the Dillon Rule.[24]

During this period, county leaders in Michigan, Nebraska, Oregon, Montana, and California were banding together in associations to share information and advocate for increased autonomy. In 1911, the California state legislature became the first one in the country to grant home rule to counties by amending its constitution.[25]

By 1935, as the Roosevelt administration was turning out national programs, George F. Breitbach, the clerk of Milwaukee County, Wisconsin, thought that a national association might be a more effective advocate for county government. He convened a meeting in Chicago, and the National County Officers Association was born. In time, this group, and the National Association of County Officials, would become the present day National Association of Counties (NACo).[26]

Legally prohibited from using public money to fund its activities, the association began selling subscriptions to its magazine, *The County*

Officer. The first national meeting was sparsely attended, but in 1939, the second meeting drew a large crowd.[27] At the tail end of World War II, the association made three decisions that would serve as the foundation of the modern incarnation of NACo. An office was opened in Washington, D.C., a law firm was retained to represent association interests, and a recruitment drive would attempt to sign up every county in the United States.[28]

It was a fortuitous moment for these decisions because fate was about to smile on those who understood the value—and wished to expand—county government.

With the war over, 12.5 million veterans had to be reintegrated into society.[29] Essential to reintegration was housing, which was addressed by no-money-down mortgages for veterans, and these VA Home Loans financed much of the explosion in suburban growth. In ten years alone, the suburbs grew by 46 percent.[30]

These homes, according to William J. Levitt, who changed the face of America with his vast suburban housing developments, could even boast a political dimension. Referring to the anxieties of the Cold War and the burgeoning American fear of communism, Levitt said, "No man who owns a house and lot can be a communist because he has too much to do."[31]

True enough, but missing from these newly built Edens were the basic services taken for granted in cities, starting with police and fire departments.[32] By the 1960s, this void was being filled by county government. According to a survey distributed by the federal government, 40 percent of counties were handling police duties, 27 percent were in charge of the jails, 37 percent were overseeing libraries, and 20 percent had taken on a broad range of functions from repairing roads to welfare.[33]

Naturally, with all of these added responsibilities, counties sought to increase their authority. Just as important was to ensure that when decisions were being debated by cities, states, and the federal government, counties would have the opportunity to express their needs and shape the outcome.[34]

However, home rule was still hard to come by. In 60 years, only 15 states had granted it to their counties. That started to change in 1970. Progress was slow until county leaders noticed the advantages of home rule and began to seek charter authority.[35]

A quarter-century later, 79 percent of 47 states have extended home rule to 2,300 counties.[36]

**

The National Association of Counties has moved well beyond George Breitbach's bravest dreams, serving some 40,000 county elected officials and 3.6 million county employees. Despite the growth, the association is continuing the work George began, advocating on behalf of counties with the federal government, sharing information, training leaders, and clarifying the mission of county government to the public. The next frontier for NACo will be fostering more cooperation among governments at every level. The issues are not suited for single players. Rather, they require partnerships, and the association is hoping to craft a new federalism, which was explained by Matthew Chase to Congress in July 2019. His testimony is reprinted in the appendix of this book.

Ironically, even as we head into the future, today's county government owes more to the eighteenth century than to the complexities of the present hour. It is the living embodiment of Thomas Jefferson's observation that the government closest to the people governs best. The phrase rings with Jeffersonian elegance, yet there is a plainer way of stating it that accounts for its effectiveness: local officials are the most personally and publicly responsible for their decisions.

How could it be otherwise? Local officials live and work in the communities they serve. Their decisions—to raise taxes, for example—impact their next-door neighbors and the mothers and fathers they meet in their child's classroom on parent-teacher night. They see their decisions play out firsthand, and of course, they hear about them—sometimes with words of praise, other times not.

Now, county officials have their own book and you can hear their voices—the challenges they face, the joys of their jobs, and the poignancy.

There is the commissioner in Washington state, working tirelessly to stem the flood of opioids into her county, establishing treatment programs, speaking to journalists, friends, and strangers who approach her, telling them about the son she lost to drugs.

You will hear from the commissioner in Nebraska trying to set up programs for the elderly all while caring for her mother with Alzheimer's and her father with cancer.

Then there is the supervisor in California dealing with the COVID-19 pandemic in a district where a large percentage of the residents do not speak English. Her struggle is to provide technology and get them the information they need in Spanish.

And the longtime executive in Kentucky, who discovered the essence of local government in the grocery store, reminding himself whenever he went shopping that he should go to the frozen-food section last because it was not uncommon for him to be waylaid by a constituent for a thirty-minute conversation before he could get to the checkout counter.

Notes

1   Rebecca Fraser, *The Mayflower: The Families, the Voyage, and the Founding of America* (New York: St. Martin's Press, 2017). p. 72.

2   Fraser, p. 43.

3   William Bradford, "The Project Gutenberg eBook, Bradford's History of 'Plimoth Plantation," 110, www.gutenberg.org/files/24950/24950-h/24950-h. htm, Retrieved August 9, 2022.

4   "The Mayflower Compact: The first governing document of Plymouth Colony," www.mayflower400uk.org/education/who-were-the-pilgrims/2019/november/ the-mayflower-compact-the-first-governing-document-of-plymouth-colony, Retrieved August 9, 2022.

5   Rachel Looker, "Origin of counties dates back to 1600s," *County News: National Association of Counties*, VOL. 51, NO. 14, July 8, 2019, p. 9.

6   Fraser, p. 55.

7   Elbridge Gerry, "Letter to the Massachusetts State Legislature Explaining His Reasons for Not Signing the Constitution," www.digitalhistory.uh.edu/disp_textbook.cfm?smtID=3&psid=4519, Retrieved August 12, 2022.

8   Richard Labunski, *James Madison and the Struggle for the Bill of Rights* (New York: Oxford University Press, 2006). p. 63.

9   U.S. Constitution, Tenth Amendment, Cornell Law School, Legal Information Institute, www.law.cornell.edu/constitution/tenth amendment, Retrieved August 12, 2022.

10   Peter Kotowski, "Whiskey Rebellion," *The Digital Encyclopedia of George Washington*, www.mountvernon.org/library/digitalhistory/digital-encyclopedia/article/whiskey-rebellion/#1, Retrieved August 14, 2022.

11   Leo Damrosch, *Tocqueville's Discovery of America* (New York: Farrar, Straus and Giroux, 2010). p. 112.

12   Damrosch, p. 138.

13   Art Swift, "Majority in U.S. Say Federal Government Has Too Much Power," Gallup, October 5, 2017, //news.gallup.com/poll/220199/majority-say-federal-government-power.aspx, Retrieved September 15, 2022.

14   United States Census Bureau, 1860 Fast Facts, www.census.gov/history/www/ through the_decades/fast_facts/1860_fast_facts.html, Retrieved September 15, 2022.

15   United States Census Bureau,1960 Fast Facts, www.census.gov/history/www/through the_decades/fast_facts/1960_fast_facts.html, Retrieved September 15, 2022.

16   United States Census Bureau, 1920 Overview, www.census.gov/history/www/through_the_decades/overview/1920.html, Retrieved September 15, 2022.

17   Alonzo L. Hamby, "Harry S. Truman: Domestic Affairs," UVA: Miller Center, //millercenter.org/president/truman/domestic-affairs, Retrieved September 17, 2022.

18   Chester J. Pach, Jr., "Dwight D. Eisenhower: Domestic Affairs," UVA: Miller Center, //millercenter.org/president/eisenhower/domestic-affairs, Retrieved September 17, 2022.

19   Thomas C. Hunt, "National Defense Education Act," *Encyclopedia Britannica*, August 26, 2022, //www.britannica.com/topic/National-Defense-Education-Act, Retrieved September 17, 2022.

20   H. S. Gilbertson, *The County: The "Dark Continent" of American Politics* (New York: The Knickerbocker Press, 1917). P. 66. www.gutenberg.org/files/67350/67350-h/67350-h.htm, Retrieved August 1, 2022.

21   John R. Vile, "Cooley, Thomas McIntyre," *Great American Judges: An Encyclopedia* (United States: ABC-CLIO, 2003). p. 178.

22 Tyler Craddock, "The Dillon Rule," National Association of Residential Property Managers, March 9, 2018, www.narpm.org/residential-resource/dillon-rule-legislative, Retrieved August 1, 2022.

23 Vile, p. 179.

24 *Hunter v. City of Pittsburgh*, 207 U.S. 161 (1907), //supreme.justia.com/cases/federal/us/207/161, Retrieved August 1, 2022.

25 NACo, *Serving America's Counties: A History of the National Association of Counties*, (Washington, D.C., National Association of Counties, 1999). pp. 8-9.

26 NACo, *Serving America's Counties*, p. 9.

27 NACo, *Serving America's Counties*, pp. 9-11.

28 NACo, *Serving America's Counties*, pp. 11-12.

29 Barbara Kelly, "The Suburban Revolution," *New York Times*, February 1, 1987.

30 "The American Dream: Suburbanization," //opened.cuny.edu/courseware/module/453/student/?task=3, Retrieved September 17, 2022.

31 Kelly, "The Suburban Revolution."

32 NACo, "History of County Government," p. 9.

33 NACo, "History of County Government," p. 10.

34 NACo, "History of County Government," p. 10.

35 NACo, "History of County Government," p. 12.

36 NACo, "History of County Government," p. 12.

HEALTH

SUBSTANCE USE DISORDER

Commissioner Lisa Janicki
Skagit County, Washington

"If I couldn't save Patrick, maybe I could contribute to saving another mother's child by telling his story and mine."

There he was, my son, Patrick, in a hospital bed, only thirty years old, and gone after lingering for two weeks in a coma.

Shocking? Unbelievable? Tragic? All three.

Patrick had struggled with drug addiction for a decade and though I knew it was irrational, I felt as if I should have saved him.

Yet as a grieving mother on that August day in 2017, I was in a unique position. Three years earlier, after serving as the chief financial officer of Janicki Industries, an engineering and manufacturing company, I was elected to the county board of commissioners. I'd run believing that more government officials should have a business background to help plan beyond the usual one- or two-year budget cycles. Now, though, I saw another opportunity. The three commissioners on the board also function as the board of health, and in that role, I would have a chance to spare others our heartbreak.

Skagit County, with a population at just under 130,000, has its share of drug problems. Overdose deaths doubled in the wake of the COVID-19 pandemic. No surprise given the isolation and depression and that two of the most popular drugs are also two of the deadliest—oxycodone and fentanyl.

I spoke to commissioners from all over the country and heard about their approaches to substance use. The thing about opioid addiction is it doesn't matter what political party you are. We all want to keep our family and community safe.

KEY STATS

Counties provide services and support to the approximately one in five adults who have a behavioral health condition such as mental illness and/or substance use disorder.

The Skagit Board enacted programs to provide—free of charge—Narcan, a drug that counters opioid overdoses, and the training on how to administer it; a syringe exchange; needle cleanup kits; a secure way for people to dispose of leftover medications; connections to treatment services; and fentanyl test strips, which are used to determine if street drugs like cocaine or heroin contain fentanyl, a few grains of which can kill an adult.

I saw another way to help. If I couldn't save Patrick, maybe I could contribute to saving another mother's child by telling his story and mine.

I had a platform beyond my seat on the board. I've lived in Skagit County for the last thirty-eight years. I was raised in Alaska and met my husband Mike while we were students at Gonzaga University. His family has deep roots here. Four generations have worked in the timber business; Janicki Industries is the largest private employer in the county. All five of our children were well known in the community. Patrick's memorial service in the Cascade Middle School gymnasium and his funeral Mass at Immaculate Conception Church were packed.

I began to speak to groups, to journalists, to friends, to strangers who came up to talk to me. I even wrote an essay for a magazine. One story that has stayed with me was my conversation with a friend whose thirty-year-old daughter was in the hospital. She had overdosed on opioids and her heart was failing. I sat with my friend and her ex-husband in the waiting room, offering words of comfort and encouraging them to talk to their daughter before it was too late. I never in a thousand years thought this young woman would survive. But she did, and her parents, who had gone through a contentious divorce, came together to support her. Later, they told me she'd had a baby and was living a clean life. I still get goosebumps thinking about it.

During my interactions with people, I heard stories of addiction and the shame that often accompanies it. Shame leads to silence, a primary roadblock to addicts asking for help. That shame is rooted in the cliché of drug addicts—men and women from troubled families, wandering the streets, committing crimes to support their habits. In some cases that is true, but not in all, and certainly not in Patrick's. His story proved that if addiction could overpower him, it had the potential to overpower anyone.

In 2007, Patrick was at a county fair climbing a pole during a logging demonstration when he fell and broke his back. The neurosurgeon said Patrick would have been face down on a bed letting his vertebrae heal if he hadn't been in excellent shape—he was a former wrestler who had qualified for the state tournament four years running. Instead, Patrick wore a metal-framed brace that allowed him to attend classes. Before he left for college in Spokane, I remember saying, "Patrick, take care of your back and do what the doctor tells you because if you don't, you'll regret it when you're forty."

Patrick returned in the summer. I'd see the pill bottles in his room and a box of fentanyl patches. I didn't know what they were, but they had prescription labels from our doctor. I wish I'd recognized the risks of that medication. I would give anything to go back and intervene.

By the fall of 2016, Patrick had fought a decade-long battle against back pain, and he informed us that he was addicted to prescription pain pills and was entering treatment. I was shocked but encouraged by his responsible decision. And I was optimistic. Patrick was his usual upbeat self; he had a good job, plenty of friends, and a supportive family.

After five weeks in treatment, Patrick came home. He attended several meetings a week with his support group. But outrunning addiction is tricky, and by the following summer, Patrick took what he thought was an OxyContin pill and went into cardiac arrest. The pill wasn't Oxy. Even after a toxicology screen, we didn't know what it was. We do know that it cost Patrick his life.

Since then, I've discovered a lot of families have dealt with this, very quietly. And that quiet, I believe, is the enemy.

There were a set of ballfields owned by the Sedro-Woolley School District. Patrick always thought there should be a playground by the fields because the youngest siblings were often left waiting for their brothers and sisters to finish their games and the little kids had nothing to do. Patrick had been a Rotarian, and to honor him the Sedro-Woolley Rotary Club, in conjunction with the school district, built that playground, a million-dollar investment in the community. It's named Pat's Playground at Janicki Fields. A sign board with Patrick's story has been put up along with another sign board directed at parents who have questions about substance use and a QR code so they can reach out for assistance.

It does my heart good driving by the playground. At the dedication, we printed up sunglasses that say *Pat's Playground* along the stems. I keep a basket of the glasses in my car and I take them to the parents and the children when they're out there on a sunny day. I tell them I'm Pat's mom and share his story.

Our more formal efforts in the county are geared toward education. First and foremost, we want to underscore that addiction is not a moral failing, and it's every bit as much a disease as cancer. To deal with it, families shouldn't blame the addict or themselves. We have a program, Skagit Rising, that educates our children, a collaborative effort between our local hospital and the school district.

At the direction of the board of health, we put together an addiction symposium in partnership with the Swinomish tribe because they are also battling addiction. We registered 550 participants, an impressive turnout. We discussed the science of addiction, particularly the changes in the brain, and we had a number of people in recovery talking about their journey through addiction. The tribe has now built a recovery and wellness center that treats more than 500 people, mostly non-tribal.

What we need to fix going forward is the shortage of counseling.

That is a huge part of the problem. It shouldn't take a four-year degree in psychology plus a doctorate to become a licensed counselor. I've advocated for a shorter educational path in order to receive a certificate to qualify. Skagit Valley College, our local community college, could be our starting point because they have a nursing program. There has been some pushback, mainly because it's new. The answer is to involve the state to define the role. In the wake of COVID-19, we know there is an immediate need to expand the capacity for counseling services. We are seeing that need in the schools and the community, and we know if people don't receive treatment, odds are good they will self-medicate, and that translates into more substance use and even deaths—unnecessary deaths.

I suppose information, whether through programs or counseling, is utmost in my mind because I still can't stop wondering if our family could have avoided losing Patrick if only we'd better understood the disease.

LOCAL HEALTH DEPARTMENTS

Board President Toni Preckwinkle
Cook County, Illinois

"If we are going to make real changes in reducing the levels of violence in our communities, we must invest in them."

Early in my professional life, I was a history teacher in Englewood, and one of my students was killed in a drive-by. She was sitting on her front porch, happened to be in the wrong place at the wrong time, and it cost the young woman her life. The tragedy cast a shadow over the school. This was more than forty years ago. The yearbook was dedicated to her, but there was no counseling for the students or the teachers. After her murder, we just went on with life, which led me to understand the importance of accessible trauma care. Later, during the nearly two decades I served as an alderman, I attended a number of funerals of young people killed in our streets. It was always heartbreaking, but it reinforced my commitment to ensuring that young people have the resources they need to avoid gun violence or to cope with its aftermath in a holistic way.

I was elected to the board of commissioners in 2010, and the head of our Health Committee insisted early on that the board pass a resolution declaring that violence was also a public health crisis in the county. We not only passed that resolution in Cook County, but we also brought it to the National Association of Counties (NACo) annual conference to ask for support, and we secured it. According to our NACo resolution, gun violence is a public health crisis in the United States.

In Cook County, we have a level of gang activity that is tragically

PETER GOLDEN

problematic and part of a national trend. Nationally, a recent report noted that gun homicides have increased by 35 percent. There were over 1,000 gun-related homicides in Cook County in 2021. That's one challenge—street organizations.

KEY STATS

Counties invest more than $100 billion in community health and hospitals annually.

The other is that we are the wrongful-conviction capital of the country, and there is a real challenge around police accountability, particularly in communities of color. When people don't have confidence in the police, they're less likely to work with them to try to solve crimes. That has extremely negative consequences, both for the residents and the police.

Half of our budget goes to public health and approximately another 30 percent to public safety—that's the court system and our jail. We treat victims of gun violence and prosecute the perpetrators. We have a unique relationship with the U.S. Navy Medical Corps. The Navy sends people to hone their skills in our emergency room because we're so adept at treating trauma.

We knew how to deal with the downstream effects of the violence, but in 2013, the board of commissioners took on violence prevention, restorative justice, and anti-recidivism efforts. We began to fund community-based organizations then and have continued to do so with our American Rescue Plan money. We put aside over $100 million for equity and justice initiatives and $75 million for violence prevention. With the American Rescue Plan resources, we really have been able to ramp up our investments in those arenas.

I've been to organizations which serve people who are just coming out of jail or prison and try to help them make the transition back into their communities. This means providing behavioral health services and support, assistance in finding employment and housing, and everything needed for returning residents. There are organizations that do restorative justice work that try to bring alleged perpetrators and victims together outside of the criminal justice system to see if we can address the harm that has been done. And we support organizations that work with at-risk youth. We cover a broad spectrum, but the unifying factor is we're trying to prevent violence and support people who are coming out of our jails and prisons and help them get on a path to productive membership in society.

Gun violence is only one measure of the challenges that many communities of color confront. Substance use and addiction are another. More people in Cook County succumbed to overdoses than were victims of violent crime in 2021. Overdoses rarely receive the same media attention as the gun violence, but it is unquestionably a comparable challenge. Our health system is responsible for dealing with both. We treat people who need care as a result of their addiction as well as people who need care as a result of being victims of violence.

Until very recently, we haven't had a very good footprint in behavioral health. One of the things that we are going to do with our American Rescue Plan resources is create a department of behavioral health services. Our first step will be taking an inventory of where we are with these services and figure out what the county needs to do to fill in the gaps. I know we have a great need for beds for people who are in crisis, particularly for juveniles.

There is a program, Healing Hurt People-Chicago, formed by the John H. Stroger, Jr. Hospital of Cook County, the University of Chicago Medicine's Comer Children's Hospital, and the Center for Nonviolence and Social Justice at Drexel University in Philadelphia. When gunshot victims come into the hospital, the program tries to provide them with wraparound services, physical and behavioral, and works to help them recognize the factors that led to the shooting and how such an outcome can be avoided in the future. This is a perfect example of the kind of program required to support victims and their families, and we need more of them.

But the challenge for our health and hospital system is that we provide a disproportionate amount of charity care. There are over sixty hospitals in Cook County. Two of those are public hospitals, and they provide half the charity care in the entire county. We'd like our academic and for-profit institutions to step up and help us by providing more care. Hopefully, we're in an environment now where that will, in the near future, be the case.

We're committed to addressing the root causes of the problems we're facing in the community. If we are going to make real changes in reducing the levels of violence in our communities, we must invest in them. I always say if you look at the high levels of poverty along with the levels of education, underperforming schools, and food deserts, it's all the same map. It's all the same communities dealing with a multitude of challenges.

And what that reflects is historic disinvestment and marginalization by the larger society. It's not a surprise that these are the communities with the highest levels of violence and struggle with substance use and so on because the larger society has kicked these communities to the curb. One of the things we have to do with our American Rescue Plan resources is invest in those communities so that we can level the playing field by making substantial investments, and we're doing that in small businesses and in housing assistance and social services.

We are also proceeding with the Guaranteed Income Pilot Program. At $42 million, it will be the largest guaranteed income pilot in the country. We have tried a lot of things in this country to help people who are in poverty, but the most obvious thing you can do for impoverished people is give them money.

We are also going to address bankruptcy because the reason working people often find themselves in that situation is that they can't pay their medical bills. The healthcare system turns its unpaid bills over to collection agencies, and if we go into that market, we can buy the debt for pennies on the dollar and give people a clean slate. We've set aside $12 million for the Medical Debt Relief Initiative. It is one of most innovative parts of our planned American Rescue Plan expenditures.

In the end, we will continue to keep working on violence prevention, anti-recidivism efforts, and the health of the residents who call Cook County home.

MENTAL HEALTH

Supervisor James Gore
Sonoma County, California

"I see a lesson in this for my community. It doesn't just need a rallying cry. It also needs a deep breath."

In California and, by extension, in Sonoma County, we have managed healthcare, yet our counties act as a safety net for mental-health services. We oversee the budget for the sheriff, human services, district attorney, and public defender departments. Therefore, we manage all the conservatorship programs—the bureaucracy of mental health and direct services. We also provide most of the contracts to community organizations that focus on mental health, including everything from upstream diversion and peer support programs, all the way to the toughest end of it—dealing directly with the most acute needs.

Our region's three main hospital networks are generally not ideal systems for managing mental health patients. The sad fact of the matter is that such care doesn't pay well, so it doesn't attract meaningful investment or interest. A lot of that work falls to us, and it's a big issue we face with our hospitals. There is a continuous negotiation with them, basically an attempt at partnership, but it does not always pay off.

Unfortunately, like many communities across the country, our largest mental-health facility is the county jail. In our case, the average daily population of our jail breaks down to 40 percent homeless, 50 percent diagnosed with mental-health issues, and half of those requiring direct, mental-health intervention. In other words, they belong in a hospital or community-based care, but are in a cell instead. Still, our hospitals remain adamant that mental health is predominantly the county's role. And we remain just as adamant that health insurance and direct providers should invest in upstream diversion programs. In the meantime, the mentally unwell often sit in jail.

KEY STATS

Within a given year, 45 percent of adults with mental illness receive treatment.

In response to these challenges, our board of supervisors created ACCESS Sonoma—Accessing Coordinated Care and Empowering Self Sufficiency. This is our county safety net system designed to deliver services to the neediest among us—those struggling financially or from substance use disorder, burdened by physical or mental disabilities, lacking housing, leaving incarceration, or suffering from some form of social inequity. As part of ACCESS, we analyze who needs the services and how best to make certain they receive them. Through data sharing, we coordinate care across our departments.

Complicating the usual assortment of challenges is that there is no shortage of natural traumas in Sonoma County. During the last decade, our climate conditions have changed drastically. In 2017, our first mega fire burned down 7,000 structures here. It caught us by surprise and knocked us back on our heels. You can't talk about that fire without mentioning the other five fires since then; the two horrendous floods in the last five years; or the ongoing twelve-year drought and what it's like to live with water curtailments and non-voluntary conservation requirements. Add all of that to over two years of the COVID-19 pandemic, and you can understand why we speak in terms of accumulative trauma and why residents are on edge, waiting for the next disaster, and how this grinds down mental health, which of course has a deleterious impact on physical health.

In general, the fires have been the hardest event for people to cope with, harder even than the pandemic. Along with the cycle of flood and drought, the viticulture industry has been damaged, which destroyed a huge joy for so many of our residents, replacing it with fear, and hurt our tourist industry. As a result, we pulled together a wildfire mental-health collaborative. The board of supervisors provided some funding, but these were mainly federally funded health clinics with some nonprofit organizations also involved. People usually come to county government last, but we did promote the collaborative effort. They have therapists and offer online personal assessment and different degrees of services depending on the acuity of the situation.

I have had to focus quite a bit on my own self-care and the care of my family. In my own life I have modeled the things I want to see in my community. Not long ago, during the pandemic, a school superintendent observed that the majority of the fourth graders in our school system had never completed a full year of school without major interruption. And it hit me: my daughter was in the fourth grade. I recalled that when she was in kindergarten, school was canceled for three weeks because of the Tubbs Fire. The next year school was closed because there was so much smoke in the air from the Butte Fire, which occurred east of us. The smoke blew into our community, and the air quality was so horrible the children had to wear masks. When my daughter was in second grade, we had the Kincade Fire, which forced us to evacuate 40 percent of our community, and my daughter probably missed two weeks of school. And then we had the COVID-19 pandemic, including two years of anxiety and interruptions. God willing, 2022 will be my daughter's first full year of school.

When talking to your children, making sure they know not to be overly afraid when they have to evacuate their home is now a requirement of parenting in our county. Personally, we've had to evacuate our house three times. We have had to set up our lives so that we are prepared: fire-hardening our house, packing a go-bag, knowing where the important documents and valuables are stored, and which photographs and keepsakes we want to take with us. We know what is important and what could burn down and be replaced by insurance. The adults must try their best to make peace with this difficult reality and help their children do the same.

In the wake of the wildfires in 2017, I reached a point where I was burnt out, pun intended, for the first time in my life. I had been the guy who was rallying everybody, doing the community organizing with the people who lost their homes, putting my staff on the ground, making general plan amendments to our county codes, changing permitting processes, relentlessly driving for us to change our system to be ready for the next fire season, testing our public warning systems, identifying flaws in our processes, meeting with the press, owning the mistakes on behalf of my board as the chair. You name it. I was up for it and I was so focused on emergency management that I was becoming very brittle and edgy.

In the past, I had been in therapy and worked on my issues in a proactive way to be healthy. I say that openly. Now, once again, I leaned in and went back to counseling and started to work through my discomfort. Not because I was in the midst of a crisis, but from the perspective that I'm healthy but wearing thin and I need to address it. So, I made the time for self-care, meditation, prayer, and took care of myself and my wife and children. I see a lesson in this for my community. It doesn't just need a rallying cry. It also needs a deep breath. We have accomplished a great deal, and we are safer than we have ever been, but emotionally we are still vulnerable.

The first step is to talk about that vulnerability. It's amazing to me that in a community that has dealt with so much trauma that some continue to resist talking about the emotional fallout. And I'm in a very aware, engaged, open-minded community. Destigmatizing the discussion of mental health is among our biggest challenges, a conclusion I reached from personal experience. Anxiety and depression ran through my family for generations. With that came self-medication in the form of alcoholism or what we called, mommy-be-calm pills—Valium. I'm not just talking about my generation, but my parents' and grandparents' generations as well. The problems weren't discussed—the attitude was "suck it up" and "deal with it." Sharing painful stories remains a tough task, but I want my children's generation to assign no stigma to these discussions, and I want the same openness to exist in my community.

Looking forward, I feel strongly that Sonoma County is on the right track, heading to a place of maturity, a place where we don't respond to the first scent of smoke with fear, but with awareness and understanding of who we are and our surroundings and how we can live with the unpredictably of nature and its sometimes-cruel aftermath. Instead of being overwhelmed by our desire to flee, we will be ready whatever comes our way, and be calm in that readiness. To me, all the dramatic changes to our system of dealing with natural disasters—the $60 million we're investing in home hardening and the insurance companies that are signing on with us to award these allocations—all of it is designed to increase our belief that even though we are confronting chaotic times, we can handle this. And I think that ability comes from the inner strength of people, not just from plans drawn up by emergency departments.

COVID-19

Supervisor Nora Vargas
San Diego County, California

"A huge lesson I took away from my experience mitigating the impacts of the pandemic, one that will guide my decision-making in the future, is the importance of engaging a community from the beginning with open communication."

When I imagined running for the county board of supervisors, I never thought my campaign would be transformed into a full-time effort to mitigate the impacts of COVID-19 in the community.

In the winter of 2020, I was in a race to become the first Latina supervisor for the County of San Diego in its 171-year history. For nearly three decades, I have been advocating locally and nationally for the community in my capacity as a former executive with Planned Parenthood and as a governing board member of Southwestern College. The district in San Diego that I hoped to represent, in the southernmost part of the county, has a population of about 630,000 and nearly 60 percent of the population is Latino. For many years, the district, mainly comprised of working families and small businesses, has historically been under-resourced and underserved. Many of our families lack access to healthcare and housing and face food insecurity.

After twenty years at Planned Parenthood, I had seen enough inequity in the healthcare system and I wanted to make a difference. I ran as a public healthcare advocate because I truly believe health is the foundation for a thriving community and a healthy economy. It was shortly after New Year's 2020 that I started hearing about this strange virus going around. No one knew much about it, and while I have a sister who is a physician, she didn't mention anything alarming.

It was in February of that year that we really started hearing about COVID-19 and the first confirmed cases in San Diego were reported. During this time, I remained president of the Southwestern College Board, and the safety of the campus community including faculty and staff was my top priority. In order to continue providing the education our students needed during this challenging time, we made sure that every student had access to computers and the internet. We were one of the first community colleges to go virtual. We converted our parking lots to Wi-Fi access points. Additionally, knowing that a significant number of our students faced food insecurity, we created a food pantry on campus, the Jag Kitchen, which was staffed by volunteers. It helped to ensure that our students did not have to worry about where their next meal was coming from.

By then, still in the midst of my campaign, it became apparent that the county needed to address the economic impact of COVID-19 on small businesses and nonprofit organizations, especially the groups that served the most vulnerable residents. I brought together a coalition of local leaders and we began having those conversations to identify what economic recovery would look like for our safety net organizations. We surveyed the communities to assess their needs and we found out that the biggest need was economic relief. Many members of the community weren't working and some received limited amounts of assistance. We found out that a lot of our children were only receiving food from school and, with the schools closed because of COVID-19, they would have no access to meals. We pushed the legislature, and we drastically increased the food stipend for families in need in the form of the pandemic EBT card which ensured our kids were not hungry.

Early on, we identified that language was a huge barrier since a large percentage of the residents in the district didn't speak English. To help deliver life-saving information, I developed an hour-long weekly Zoom broadcast called *Conexiones*. It was in Spanish. We would invite experts to speak on a range of topics—for example, a panel of researchers discussing vaccine hesitancy or teachers explaining how parents might talk to their young children about COVID-19. The county responded very positively.

While this was happening, my father was very ill. My sisters, brother, and I were his caretakers. He underwent dialysis three to four times a week and contracted COVID-19 twice. He was hospitalized for four months—half of that in the ICU—and none of us were allowed to visit him. He managed to survive until January 2022, but I remember his months alone in the hospital as a nightmare.

As I won my race and officially was sworn into office and became the first Latina, first immigrant, and first woman of color to serve on the board of supervisors in the history of the county, COVID-19 was continuing to spread. Our ICUs were at capacity and our healthcare system was in distress, a combination of a highly contagious virus and a shortage of healthcare workers. Another factor was that many of our community members lacked access to healthcare, so they automatically went to emergency rooms when they were sick. We knew then that we needed to implement innovative strategies and one of the first steps was to bring in our *promotoras*, which are healthcare workers who are trusted by the Latino community. The *promotoras* engaged the community and helped those most vulnerable by scheduling vaccination appointments for people without computers and did it in their language. They also helped share information with the community in their language. We also used this model to vaccinate folks in nursing homes and we created programs through our EMTs and our fire department to help with vaccinations.

At that moment in the pandemic, nobody really knew what was

happening, so our county board of supervisors created a COVID-19 subcommittee to ensure a coordinated effort across all departments and community partners. We began holding press conferences every Wednesday to inform the community about resources and support and I made sure that the message was also delivered in Spanish. As the co-chair of the subcommittee, I brought my healthcare expertise as well as my record of working closely with communities on the ground.

All these efforts received an incredible response from the community. To broaden our reach, I created the South Bay Equity and Economic Task Force that brought together stakeholders including mayors, school board members, chambers of commerce, newspaper reporters, and media producers in my district. By coming together, we assessed the different needs and barriers each community had. With the feedback, we took direct action and implemented innovative strategies to ensure that our community members had access to resources, vaccines, and the correct information.

Our community faced much uncertainty, especially the undocumented residents who were afraid of coming forward to be vaccinated, but not because they didn't trust the vaccines. They were afraid that their immigration status could be impacted. We made sure to remove these types of barriers so they had equitable access to the vaccines without fear. So, if you were an eighty-five-year-old individual who came to San Diego from Mexico as a child living with your daughter and showed up with your daughter, who could attest to your identity, you could receive a vaccine. I was really proud of that because I think it demonstrates that representation matters—that if you have elected officials who understand communities, and who can advocate for them, it makes a difference when you create policies.

In order to make sure that the most impacted communities had what they needed, our board adopted a resolution that ensured the county's response to the pandemic was equitable. This meant that decisions were based on data and resources were allocated where the need was greater. But that was not enough. Our county passed a resolution that declared racism a public health crisis to address the disparities that were exacerbated by the impacts of COVID-19.

A huge lesson I took away from my experience mitigating the impacts of the pandemic, one that will guide my decision-making in the future, is the importance of engaging a community from the beginning with open communication. Equally important is to have the right messengers delivering the message. You need trusted messengers, whether doctors or elected officials, who speak the same language as the community— messengers who stay away from politicking on social media and all that nonsense and noise because, in the end, you have to make long-term decisions for communities, not for an election or campaign.

CORONERS

Coroner Dotti Owens
Ada County, Idaho

"One tragedy that we as coroners consistently see is suicide, and I've learned to watch these like a hawk."

Ada County is home to Boise, the state capital, and provides coroner services to thirty-one of the forty-two counties in Idaho. There are lots of small counties within our state and I grew up in one of them—Jerome. The population was maybe six thousand at the time. This was so different from our current Ada County population which, because of current population increase, is now close to half a million. When I first took office, I noticed all the counties had different ways of performing death investigations throughout the state. For example, a coroner once told me, "I don't consider a Russian roulette case a suicide because it's harder on the families, and I just don't think it is." By standards, most of these types of cases are.

Once in office, I jumped into our state coroners' association with both feet. It took months, but I was eventually able to develop a state standards manual for Idaho, followed by classes which resulted in half of the state coroners achieving their certification from the American Board of Medicolegal Death Investigators (ABMDI). This certification had never been reachable for Idaho coroners, and since then we've been trying to become a teaching resource for our smaller, more rural jurisdictions.

In 2017, my office became accredited by the National Association of Medical Examiners (NAME) for the first time in the history of the county. The process was difficult and compared to earning my master's degree in two weeks. The Ada County Coroner's Office had and remains to be accredited with International Associations of Counties and Medical Examiners (IACME) since 2010. NAME was the second accreditation for my office, giving us dual accreditation status, one of six in the nation to hold both. That dual accreditation opened the door for federal grants. With grant funding opportunities, we expanded our existing space and in the late winter of 2021, because of the growth that Ada County is experiencing, a new facility was needed and we broke ground for a 40,000-square-foot coroner's facility with a completion date of October 2023.

KEY STATS

County medical examiner and coroner offices often face shortages of forensic pathologists to investigate deaths.

Budget is always a problem in county government, especially with the office of the coroner. Coroners have had minimal budgets and maximum denials for requests for funds for years. When your coroners have been in office for fifteen years, and their budget requests are routinely turned down, they quit asking. But the days of the coroner just being body transport are finished. A couple years ago, I received a phone call from a coroner who couldn't get anywhere with his commissioners during budget, and his equipment and staffing were minimal for his size county. I asked to come and do a presentation at their board meeting on the role of the coroner in our state. One thing I stressed to them—families are starting to learn that their coroners have a job to do and that there is some liability for counties for coroners not doing their jobs. What happens if you have an officer-involved shooting, and your coroner is not taking photos because his board refused to buy him a camera? I gave a lot of presentations throughout my first years as coroner and it worked. The commissioners weren't wanting to not fund these offices, they just didn't know the roles and responsibilities. They simply didn't know the job.

At that point, I started presenting at the Idaho Association of Counties and we've been able to secure more funding—education is everything. Despite efforts, we still have counties that won't budge. I have coroners who call me and say, "I need a cooler because my population has tripled" or "I need a camera or laptop." There is still lot of work ahead, but it's better than it was.

One tragedy that we as coroners consistently see is suicide, and I've learned to watch these like a hawk. Out of all the suicides in Ada County, 83 percent have consistently been middle-aged white men, between the ages of 35 to 50 years old. About five years ago, we saw our rates start climbing—growing to 125 suicides with 83 percent of them men. Obsessed with why this was happening with this demographic, I pulled the case files and read through the cases on the weekends. One commonality, men don't ask for help. They don't want to say, "I'm in trouble."

I felt like this was really going to get out of hand if I didn't do something. In the spring of 2019, I attended a conference about suicide prevention. They specifically addressed that the best way to slow these numbers down was to build a community of men that could rely on one another. They implemented Man Therapy, a pilot program in Denver designed to bring men together for events and activities such as beer and nachos, sporting events and watching sports on TV. It worked—four people turned into twenty-five and then fifty, and their suicide rate dropped. I loved the idea of this program and thought it was exactly what Ada County needs. I was able to secure a grant and contacted mantherapy.org. It's phenomenal. The website lists all the resources in your counties, who you can call, and where to go for help. They even have a "Head Inspection test" to rate your mental health status. We obtained the licensing and we've had it now for over a year. It's been huge for us. Our suicide hotline has taken critical calls that have stemmed from our Man Therapy ads.

One of the events we held was Suicide Shakedown which centered around Harleys. We had over 80 bikes show up and 250 people. I'm a big Harley fan, and Harley-Davidson donated space and helped with advertising. We teamed up with One More Day, a veteran suicide-prevention program. The rally was a ball. We'll do it again. I can't wait to see numbers and if we are making an impact. I'm hoping we can host a pool tournament or an event at a bowling alley and have one of our sporting goods stores sponsor a fishing day—anything where we bring these men together and persuade them to talk.

Suicide and the need for prevention was a problem I could think about. It was present. But COVID-19 came out of nowhere. As a coroner, I was elbows-deep in everything that had to do with COVID-19, and I was fighting those that thought deaths from the virus were fake. We were forced to buy a mass-fatality trailer to store the bodies as our facility was constantly full. So that I was 100 percent transparent, I issued a press release about the trailer. After all, it was parked outside our facility and hard to miss. I didn't want to be accused of hiding anything. I wanted everyone to see it and understand that between our population growth and COVID-19, we were getting our butts kicked. I believe that transparency is what my community deserves—be 100 percent square with them and admit when I'm wrong and take the hit, but also take the praise when I'm right.

After the press release, I started getting phone calls, tons of phone calls. People were harassing me, asking why I was lying to them about COVID-19 all while I was signing death certificates and performing autopsies on people who had diabetes or other comorbidities, and they wouldn't have died if not for the virus. A reporter from CNN reached out to me, observing that I was in a very Republican state and my position on COVID-19 was detrimental to me with the voters.

"I don't care what it does for me," I replied. "I'm doing this because I need people to understand our COVID-19 numbers are through the roof. The funeral homes are full. The VA Hospital called and said, 'We don't have any more storage. Can you help us?' Our hospitals are overflowing. And you're asking me about my job? If I don't get re-elected, I don't get re-elected. But if we can save people by speaking out, we're going to do it." After that interview, most of the harassment stopped.

My staff was wonderful during the pandemic. At the time, I had a staff of twenty-eight, and six of them got sick. Our supervisors were exhausted from covering shifts. But nobody griped and they all showed up. There might have been tears shed here and there, but we rolled on. I remember thinking, "We've got great people." That's one piece of advice I've shared with coroners—hire great people.

Another great piece of advice I give is spend time on your needs assessment. That's especially important in Idaho because we're booming. I ask county and state officials all the time: "Why aren't we growing our infrastructure to respond to our population increase?" And they always answer: "We are growing our infrastructure." My response: "Yes—fire, EMS, and law enforcement, but what are you going to do when people die? Because guess what? They're dying as fast as some of them are moving in. Your population increases, your death rate increases."

Everyone loves to increase first responder infrastructure such as fire, EMS, and law enforcement. It's community based and popular among communities. But everybody forgets that coroners are experiencing the same stuff and running our butts off. Some of the counties in Idaho have just one coroner as a part-timer that gets paid $50 for a callout. Who's going to do this job with no funding? There are four full-time coroners in the state, me being one of them. Everyone else is part-time. Because of our population increase, at least half of our forty-two counties should have a full-time coroner. I wanted to see what coroners were making around the state in comparison to the other part-time elected officials. The Idaho Association of Counties conducts a wage comparison. I compared that to the population. What I saw was that you have part-time county commissioners making $50,000 or $60,000 a year, and part-time coroners making $15,000. I then went to the National Association of Counties legislative conference in 2021. I had a resolution passed by the Health and Human Services Committee to support increased funding for needs assessments.

Now that I have it passed, I have no idea what in the hell to do with it. I'd like to develop a needs assessment for our coroner systems around the nation. I'd like to see if it is an Idaho problem or a problem everywhere. Without even looking, I know it's a national problem. Another need is a set of national standards and accreditation because there is a serious medical component to the job. If you don't want to learn it, you shouldn't be in office. If you're paid like a professional, you should be professional.

HUMAN
SERVICES

ELDERLY

Commissioner Mary Ann Borgeson
Douglas County, Nebraska

"You have to make certain that you are providing the services people want and need."

Mama had Alzheimer's disease, but Daddy was healthy enough to be her caregiver, and they happily lived in their own house. Then Daddy was diagnosed with cancer. When he had to be taken to a doctor's appointment, Mama couldn't be left alone, so I brought her with us. If he was in the hospital, I had to stay at the house with Mama because bringing her to our home confused her. It was a grueling schedule because I was also looking after my husband who was being treated for cancer. Sometimes, my husband and Daddy were at the infusion center together, not a family outing I'd wish on anyone. I did have help—Meals on Wheels, housekeeping, snow removal, and I tried a companion for Mama, but the change was too much for her to handle.

I was no stranger to healthcare. I'd been an X-ray technician, and I was born and raised in Douglas County and have been a commissioner since 1994, so I was on top of the latest developments in the county. While I was honored to be able to care for the two people who had once cared for me, I understood that not everyone who wanted to offer this care to aging parents would be in a position to do so. I also learned that caregiving takes a toll on your physical and mental well-being. You lose the balance in your life while being reluctant to ask for help and to say no to an unreasonable request. And worst of all, while you are trying your best, you ask yourself if you are doing enough.

I mention my experience because by 2038, there will be more 65-year-olds in the United States than 18-year-olds, and county governments across the country are considering how that will affect their communities and wondering if they are prepared to serve those individuals. Like my parents, most older Americans want to remain in their homes. How do we make that possible? And what about the elderly who don't have that option? What services and facilities should be available to them?

> **KEY STATS**
>
> Counties own and support over 800 nursing homes.

In Douglas County, we have a nursing home with 254 beds. In addition, we belong to a regional system created by the state that partners us with four other counties in our area. As a commissioner, we govern the services for our older residents. Federal, state, and local dollars come into the Office on Aging. We figure out which services are needed and contract with our private sector to provide them—Meals on Wheels, nursing, our homemaker program, foster grandparent program, and transportation are among our most important and expensive services. Our elderly need to get to the supermarket and the drugstore, to the hospital and their doctors' offices, and because of the expense of making it available around the clock, transportation is a major question for counties everywhere.

One of the significant problems we are dealing with is staffing—drivers, home-health aides, housekeeping, you name it—our private sector contractors are struggling to fill the growing need. The wait lists get longer. And the COVID-19 pandemic made it more challenging. Businesses shut down, and the governor ordered our public schools to move to remote learning. But county government is unique. We don't close. We just looked for new ways to provide the services and made sure our elderly received their food deliveries and medications. For doctors' visits, we used telemedicine, and to see how our residents were faring we checked in via Zoom. Technology, while not a solution to the staffing shortages, improved our outreach.

Communication is key to accomplishing this. You have to make certain that you are providing the services people want and need. You also have to stay in touch with the private providers to find out where they are running into trouble, and with your state and federal delegations to see that you have the funds to pay the providers.

Paradoxically, when it comes to caring for the elderly, the needs of urban and rural counties are the same and different. It's obvious that caregiving requires caregivers. There are more people to hire in urban counties, and this is complicated by the trend in rural counties with their increasing older population and decreasing younger population, a trend that will make the existing problem far worse. Furthermore, during the last decade, rural areas were losing the local hospitals that had wings dedicated to patients transferred from nursing homes. That means the patients have to be cared for in distant hospitals, an added stress for everyone involved. The quick daily visits so beneficial to the mood and overall health of the patients and their loved ones—particularly elderly spouses—are nearly impossible. The longer distance also adds time and money to the transports, which are already pressed for both.

One positive development—and this is going on in counties through their offices on aging—is that they have assembled a cadre of folks who can go into a situation with elderly people and assist them with any transition they are undergoing. For example, suppose a couple is living on their own in their own house or apartment. But now they are no longer able to afford to stay there; someone from the office of aging steps in and helps them look for affordable, independent housing. Then suppose later on this couple is finding their living arrangement difficult; someone comes in and evaluates them and finds they need assisted living. They help with that transition—never an easy one because the couple is giving up their lifelong independence. Finally, if necessary, they are helped with their move from assisted living to a nursing home. I can tell you from my own experience that my parents were very adamant about wanting to stay in their home. And when it comes to the time that is not feasible, it is very difficult for everyone involved. Staff at the assisted living facility and the nursing home can also lend a hand, but this only works because there is a solid partnership between providers and local government.

Counties have had success establishing these public-private partnerships within their communities. The array of services I've mentioned would not have been possible without these partnerships. These types of partnerships will remain important as we move into the future in Douglas County and in counties across our country.

Due to the sheer number of our aging populations, our biggest challenge remains finding the people to hire. For instance, there is a nursing shortage in hospitals and long-term care facilities. We are going to have to put our heads together with our educational institutions to discover how we can partner with them and show the kids that there are good-paying, fulfilling jobs for them if they receive the proper training.

My final word on this situation is a reminder. With the advances in medicine, more and more Americans will live longer lives, and in the end, elder care is something your parents or neighbors will need. If you are blessed to live a long life, in all likelihood you will need these services as well.

CHILDREN

**Children's Developmental Services
Agency Director Lisa Cloninger**
Mecklenburg County, North Carolina

"It is easy to get discouraged ... and the cure for that discouragement is among the greatest services we offer—hope for a better tomorrow."

When I was going to school for my master's degree in social work, my sister gave birth to a child with a disability. As an aunt, I had the chance to feel and witness a little bit of what parents go through in this situation—the testing and waiting and anxiety and helplessness. My nephew ended up being diagnosed with a rare genetic disorder. With not a lot of children around with the same diagnosis, I watched his parents search for information and doctors and saw, firsthand, the highs and lows of how people in this predicament are treated by healthcare professionals.

I was in the midst of job hunting, and this experience definitely sealed the deal for me. I knew I wanted to work with kids with disabilities and I thought: I love infants and toddlers, and I have this nephew who will need early-intervention services and support in school. I had some insight into how all of that would fit together and how this journey impacted my sister and her family.

One disheartening aspect I noted as I began working—and this was pre-pandemic—is that even though we're lucky in Mecklenburg County because we're a resource-rich area, our process for working with young children and families is fairly siloed. Plenty of programs do a particular piece of the work, and it's hard sometimes to get the programs to share information with each other about how they work together to serve families. Multiple programs may touch a family for a variety of reasons, but due to a lack of communication, everyone involved winds up thinking that somebody else is doing the work, and the reality is they're not and the work doesn't get done. Or it could be they are all duplicating some service while other needs aren't being met.

KEY STATS

Counties invest $62.8 billion annually in federal, state, and local funds in human services while serving as the front-line social safety net.

Countering the siloing of services has been an overarching challenge over the course of my career. Another major challenge is finding the opportunities to hear from parents about the continuity of services they need. Our programs serve children from birth until their third birthday. That's a very limited amount of time, yet we know that children with significant disabilities will require long-term care and support, particularly once they are old enough to go to school. Mecklenburg is a big county with a big school system that features one of the largest programs in the state. We are trying our best to train parents on how to access the specific systems that will meet their child's needs, all while talking to families and listening to what they really need.

One of the main ways our program helps is through service coordination—the best answer to the siloing of services. A coordinator is connected with a family when they first enter the system. The coordinator walks them through the whole process and checks in on a regular basis. Occasionally, staff leave us or change roles, but we try to keep the originally assigned person involved with the family so they really learn the needs and concerns. Staff have trained in how to provide evidence-based resources to their clients, and over time they teach the families how to access services and solve problems on their own. Our time with families is short term so we are always looking toward the future with them. After a child's third birthday, if ongoing services are needed, the school system becomes the means for early intervention.

One of our most important functions is case management. We tailor our support to the child—we serve children with developmental delays and medical issues that can cause lifelong challenges like Down syndrome, autism, and vision and hearing loss. We are fortunate that we get to interact with parents, often right as their child is being born. The COVID-19 pandemic forced us to provide services virtually, and when the worst of it had passed, it changed the way we dealt with extremely premature newborns and medically fragile children who need to be out and about in the community.

Managing the cases enables us to provide developmental evaluations and assessments. Those assessments help families identify their needs and keep track of their child's development—where they are making progress and doing well and where they may need more support. Then we link them with providers like physical therapists, occupational therapists, speech therapists, and mental-health providers, any of the folks they may require. We provide a good transition and a warm handoff by teaching them how to get ready for school and how to navigate those services. I occasionally go on home visits with staff so that I can see what the interactions look like. I am in an administrative role now, but I do see children outside of this job and families of preschoolers and older children who aren't connected with this program. All of this helps me stay grounded and to evaluate the services we offer.

One constant problem we face is identifying children who can utilize our help. Sometimes children get funneled into private therapy services because their parents don't find out about us. As a county organization, we don't have the funding to advertise. It is hard to make contact with families where Spanish, not English, is their first language. We have done a lot of work to find these families and made some headway by hiring bilingual staff, and now some 35 percent of our annual referrals each year come from Spanish-speaking families.

To increase our reach, we have established community collaborations. We have good relationships with both hospital systems here in Charlotte. They know our eligibility criteria and talk with families when a child meeting our criteria is born. The other group we collaborate with is

Youth and Family Services. Once they have documented that a child under three has been abused or neglected or in any way is in need of our services, the social workers make a referral to us. We also have strong relationships with developmental pediatricians who see many children in our age group, and we have regular communications with the doctors to make sure they understand how to send referrals to us.

Paying attention to the mental-health and social-emotional needs of young children and their families has always been a piece of our program, but lately we have really dug in on this, making sure our staff is well trained. We have a large group of mental-health clinicians licensed to do individual and family therapy, but the need for this is tremendous and continues to expand, and our plan in the years to come is to expand with it. We are getting several staff trained in an evidence-based practice called child-parent psychotherapy. We're excited that we're going to offer that service. Nobody else in the county offers this service to young children. We're proud that we can, and we want to keep increasing that capacity.

Overall, we're working to be more mindful of toxic stress and its impact on young children's brain development and on families in general, and we are devising strategies to assist families on this specific issue while they are receiving our services. I think that continues to be a challenge in society as a whole, so it's important for us to manage these types of stressors. Sometimes we think when there is family stress, it doesn't impact the baby or the little ones as much as it impacts older children. The truth is, in my view, it is really quite the opposite. We are trying to educate families about that and the very simple ways to build attachment and to repair attachment, a necessary skill particularly for the children in our program who have been in foster care and are going back home to their parents.

Doing this work, with children and families facing challenges most of us would have trouble imagining, it is easy to get discouraged. Yet I have been here for twenty years, and the cure for that discouragement is among the greatest services we offer—hope for a better tomorrow.

HOMELESSNESS

Council Chair Derek Young
Pierce County, Washington

"All of us have problems and the outcome is often a question of who has a hand to help lift them up. Not everyone has that hand, so the rest of us are obligated to be there for them."

I grew up here, on the shore of Puget Sound. In 1997, at the age of twenty-one, I ran for the Gig Harbor City Council to prove a point and stunned everyone, including myself, by winning. When the election night celebration ended, I realized that the voters had trusted me, and I better do a damn good job. Being very young, I wasn't precisely sure what that meant, so I sought every opportunity to find out and became active with my city association. After sixteen years in office, when I was elected to the county council, I got involved with the National Association of Counties, where you can learn a good deal about serving your county.

Counties present both general and specific challenges shaped by their main industries, residents, and geography, and the primary fact of our lives is Puget Sound. I don't think you can live here and not be an environmentalist who wants to fight like hell to discourage sprawl and to protect rural lands for agriculture, timber, minerals, wildlife and its natural beauty. We were losing so much of that before passing the Growth Management Act.

However, there is a strong, anti-growth sentiment in the environmental movement that is unhealthy, and not just on the economic side. As your population increases, people have to live somewhere, so you must accept the increased density in your urban areas, and we haven't handled that well. We've had a massive influx of job seekers in the region, along with stunning economic expansion—much of it to our north in King

County, the areas around Seattle and Bellevue. We haven't built enough residential construction to keep up with the influx, which has created a housing crisis for everyone. With people frantically outbidding each other, prices are out of control. The wealthy can buy, but the shortage of modestly priced homes lands hardest on the people least able to deal with it. We went from a small, persistent population of homelessness to a full-blown crisis.

KEY STATS

Five states saw their homeless population grow in double digits in 2018.

Before COVID-19 arrived, I commuted to work on the bus, riding into Tacoma from the suburbs, and you can't miss the homeless encampments downtown. I enjoyed seeing the same people on the bus during the week. They weren't my literal friends; they were my bus friends; and talking to them I quickly understood that some of them were unhoused. It was impossible not to notice and to imagine what it must be like for them on those terrible wet nights in western Washington, or when it's unbearably hot or cold, or when smoke from the forest fires clouds the air.

In many cases, the people I encountered on the bus were simply normal folks, not the stereotypes conjured up by the word "homeless." They were trudging off to work every day, and their biggest problem, I discovered during our conversations, was a run of bad luck, a discovery that left me feeling… but before the grace of God go I. My life has been a lucky one. If I'd ever faced the same difficulties I heard about during my daily commute without a family to assist me, I may well have wound up in the same unhappy boat. Seeing myself as no different than my bus mates underscored the truth that all of us have problems and the outcome is often a question of who has a hand to help lift them up. Not everyone has that hand, so the rest of us are obligated to be there for them.

This isn't to say there aren't other causes to homelessness. Compounding our lack of affordable housing, we have a large number of people with debilitating mental-health and substance-use problems, and they no longer have a place to seek basic treatment and permanent supportive housing. It's impossible to live here and not see the vast number of homeless, but even more disconcerting is that we know there are plenty of homeless we don't see. Our cities can't deal with it on their own. It's a regional problem, and we are the regional government.

As always, we had budgetary constraints. In 2005, there were savage cuts in federal mental-health funding, and because the state didn't want to step in on its own, counties were given a local option to levy a sales tax to deal with behavioral health. Yet we were the only urban county that hadn't used that option. Passing it was one of the reasons I ran for the county council. We finally succeeded last year, and now we're making those first investments, trying to invest those dollars smartly for mental-health support and treatment for substance use, but frankly, our money doesn't match our needs.

Dealing with housing was trickier because we didn't have a dedicated funding source. Then, COVID-19 erupted and suddenly we had an influx of dollars from the federal Coronavirus Aid, Relief, and Economic Security Act and the American Rescue Plan Act. At the same time, another idea was percolating around the region—retrofitting buildings to house the homeless. Prior to the pandemic, we planned to find a facility to provide housing and a central office to provide services, so people coming out of our crisis center would have a place to stay and heal for a while until we got them on their feet and into a more regular housing arrangement. With COVID-19 spreading across the county and our additional funding combined with our local revenue, more opportunities became available, namely a hotel that had been hit hard by the pandemic. We had been renting it for anyone who had to quarantine but didn't have a safe place to isolate.

That was when we decided we should hang onto this hotel. As of today, it is still used for quarantine, but this year it will transition into permanent supportive housing. As a rule, homelessness is transitory, a brief period of crisis that doesn't happen again. It's often due to a family breakup, domestic violence, the loss of a job, those kinds of things. And you have to be ready to rehouse people on the spot and keep them until they can take care of themselves.

Then there are folks with even steeper hills to climb. It can be a physical disability or a behavioral-health issue. It's clear they won't be able to afford housing on their own for a long time. For them we are beginning to set up stabilization services. How do we get them to a place where their mental-health disorders are not causing them so much trouble? How do we help them recover from a substance-use problem? The answer is by recruiting more treatment services and creating diversion alternatives to jail.

In 2017, we launched the Mobile Community Intervention Response Team (MCIRT), a group of mental-health professionals who go out and visit people on a proactive basis. Frequently, they are referred to us by first responders or because of 911 calls. MCIRT teams work to stabilize these people and monitor them for three months to see if they have more contacts with emergency personnel. We are also setting up our police with co-responders who have de-escalation training because the last place we want to put the mentally ill is in jail.

We have made a significant investment in these undertakings, nearly $250 million in our biannual budget. We are looking for opportunities to build subsidized housing, permanent supportive housing, rapid rehousing, and mixed-use projects with mixed income levels. We're preparing to throw everything at it over the next two years, and I believe we will look at adopting the local housing tax to raise ongoing operating capital. That's important because the state has allowed us to invest a substantial amount of money that we can bond against, and that will give us money beyond the traditional methods of funding.

Despite all the impassioned news stories and speeches about homelessness and the political debates about its causes and cures, the plain fact of the matter is that we have not built enough housing for enough people in this country. We need housing at every level. And while that doesn't mean we have to allow more sprawl and destroy the beauty around us, it means that we must build with more density. That will change the way we live and the way we move around.

That may not be the answer people want to hear, but I believe it is the only answer there is.

VETERANS

**Regional Veterans Service Center
Director Cathrene Nichols**

Spokane County, Washington

*"Veterans are a special population. They gave their best effort.
We owe it to them to do the same."*

I'm a veteran of the United States Army, and I have spent my career outside of the military serving veterans. From the start, when I worked at the Washington State Department of Veterans Affairs, I fell in love with helping this very special population. I suppose I'm proudest of the fact that our county recently received a 2022 National Association of Counties Achievement Award because we've put in place some of the best county practices helping veterans in the nation. For me, it's been a dream come true and better than I could ever have imagined.

Spokane County is home to some 44,000 veterans, with another 20,000 or so when you add in all of the rural communities surrounding us. I started my job at the center in 2017. At the time, the office in Spokane was tiny and there were few long-term positive outcomes. Luckily, we have some amazing out-of-the-box thinkers among our county leadership and we had a robust budget of $1.2 million. Approximately $500,000 a year was earmarked for emergency financial assistance, primarily food and gas vouchers, and the state programs on the west side of Washington weren't really accessible to veterans on the east side of the state—if the veterans even knew the programs existed. Further complicating this problem was that the way the center was run by the previous director, it appeared that they didn't know what they didn't know. Obviously, they were assisting veterans. But when the needle wasn't moving for veteran homelessness or unemployment, people started wondering how we could do this better.

I was hired because of the institutional knowledge I gained while working for the state. I was charged with figuring out a way to use our funding for better outcomes. In the end, we came up with new policies and revamped the entire system. We hired county veteran service officers. Our region brought in over $9 million in VA claims awards. We went from an emergency financial assistance program that was providing for the basic needs of veterans to a regional veteran services center that has eight times the reach. Once we became more involved in the lives of veterans, they began securing jobs in the community instead of just sitting home and collecting a government check. An added benefit of the federal funding is that veterans who are now stable are buying homes and cars, the county receives the sales tax, and this is a significant return on investment. An even greater reward, though—and this is often overlooked—is that when we stabilize a situation for a veteran, we are also assisting that veteran's family, whether it's the spouse and children, parents or siblings who have been trying to help but lack the resources and know-how.

We have been fortunate in another way. Washington state has actively created opportunities for our county veteran officers. This is crucial. For instance, the Veterans Benefits Administration is a difficult system to navigate. You can literally find the statistical proof that veterans who file their own claims online using eBenefits are often turned down. They will send in a claim thinking that, "I hurt my back in the service and qualify for disability," but because they didn't properly word the claim or use the right codes for the diagnosis or missed any of the multiple details the VA requires, the claim is denied right out of the gate.

The county has assumed the role of advocating for veterans, which has improved the quality of life for the people we serve. We have reduced veteran homelessness in Spokane where almost everywhere else it's growing. We increased veterans' income and health benefits, and established different types of programs that help with the transition from the military to civilian life. Our service officers are cross-trained in expedited Social Security and disability application benefits, and we have partnered with WorkSource Washington, a state program that brings together companies and job seekers. The upshot of all this effort is a decreased demand for financial assistance from the community and we have reinvested the money to expand our programs.

We have a beautiful service center, very welcoming, tailor-made to honor veterans with patriotic artwork and a water wall that creates a serene environment. We have free Wi-Fi and computers accessible for them. The whole atmosphere is designed to be positive and to honor the service of our veterans. They can receive assistance with their resume. We're one-stop shopping, so to speak, a holistic approach, connecting veterans to anything they might need from jobs to healthcare. They don't have to come in the door and prove themselves. We exist because of them.

Our philosophy is based on establishing county veteran service officers—the CVSO model—which is the best arrangement for meeting the needs of the sizable number of veterans often found in large counties. The truth is that it is impossible for officials in a state capital to directly impact the lives of veterans in far-flung, mainly rural, communities. Here, we have mountains between our state government and the rest of eastern Washington.

We are serving the counties east of the Cascades—Stevens, Ferry, Pend Oreille, Whitman, Lincoln, and Grant. We even have folks crossing over from northern Idaho. In general, our service-delivery area includes all of the surrounding rural counties that must use the VA Medical Center in Spokane because we only have two VA hospitals near us. It was apparent to me from the beginning that having a regional approach was the first, necessary piece of the puzzle. We became very community oriented versus being state or federally oriented. Over time, we have created a bit of a consortium with all of the county veteran service officers in our region—all of them trained in how to deal with the government programs accessed by veterans. This, I believe, is more effective than traditional veteran organizations for three main reasons— we're streamlined; we're experienced in the complexities of negotiating the maze of government programs; and we have access to more funding, which allows us to offer decent salaries to our veteran service officers, all of whom earn accreditation through our state department of veterans' affairs.

Once we saw that our approach was successful, meaning that no one was coming back for financial assistance, we continued to case manage and walk them through the required steps to reach a sustainable outcome. We began to encourage and educate our neighboring counties. My team and I were involved in the recruitment process because the most crucial step in serving veterans is hiring the right people to help them. Then we made sure that all of our hires had the same level of high-quality training to be able to engage veterans where they are. I think that's why county government works—period—and you could make this argument for all types of services, not just those for veterans. County government is there and will always be there for the simple reason that people prefer to be served where they are. They want local people who understand their particular economy, their particular struggles, their particular culture in their community.

This past year we provided services to over 6,500 veterans. I am especially proud that throughout the COVID-19 pandemic, our center stayed connected and we did not cut back the services to our region. After five years working at the center, it has become apparent to me that an important contributing factor to our success is that we take a regional approach. The sad truth is that many rural counties—poorly funded and lacking expertise—can't do it on their own. But when they're able to partner with some of their neighboring urban counties, they wind up with more resources. One roadblock holding back other programs I've noticed is the competition among counties. Of course, part of this is due to the fact that every government program competes for funding. Yet there is an emotional component as well, a tendency to be super-proprietary—let's call it county tribalism. However, when all is said and done, collaboration will be better for both the counties and the veterans, and the proof of that is the increased quality of attention the veterans receive.

As I reflect on my experience, I'd love to see that spirit of collaboration take hold among county leaders across the nation. Veterans are a special population. They gave their best effort. We owe it to them to do the same.

IMMIGRATION

Supervisor Manuel "Manny" Ruiz
Santa Cruz County, Arizona

"While we can't solve the challenge of immigration reform locally, it's local government that has a far clearer picture of the challenges and rewards."

My father taught me to dream. It's the most important gift I ever received.

In the 1950s, Dad had his own business in Mexico. He was clearing $20 a day, decent money in those years. He exchanged that to come to the city of Nogales, our county seat, and work for 50 cents an hour. Why? Because he could imagine a better life for his children. He's 96; my mom is 89. All Dad had in Mexico was a second-grade education, but he's the smartest man I know, and he always says to me, "I wish I would've had the opportunity you had in school. Who knows what I could've done?"

I know what Dad did do, and I'm proud of him for it. He helped Mom raise eleven children; he built our home and worked construction. Sometimes we didn't have a lot, but we always had something to eat. I was the oldest child, and when I was a teenager, I was out there working for him. To this day there are houses he built that don't even have a single sediment crack in them. I'm 66 years old, a first-generation American, and I've lived in Santa Cruz County my whole life. When I was born, we had a population of maybe 10,000; now, we're at 50,000-plus with most of our people living in Nogales and north of here in the town of Rio Rico. It's a unique place. Most of us have family in Mexico, and it's easy to visit back and forth—at least it was until the pandemic shut the border and we had so many businesses close down.

If you brought in suburbanites from one of the coasts or the Midwest and they looked out from downtown Nogales, I can imagine what they would see—a dry, hilly, unforgiving land where it gets blazing hot in the summer and dips to freezing in the winter.

KEY STATS

County leaders are important stakeholders in discussions related to federal immigration policies.

Yet that's not what my father saw, nor is it what I and the Mexican families see when we look past the steel fence and razor wire that separates the United States from Mexico. All of us see the same thing: that land just across the Mexican border where dreams still come true.

There are three ports of entry in Nogales: Dennis DeConcini, Nogales-Mariposa, and Morley Gate. Once across the border, everything you can think of seems to flow north: storm water, wastewater, drugs, and illegal immigrants.

When I was first elected, illegal immigration was not my most glaring problem. It was that they would find remains in the outlying areas of Nogales, and it cost the taxpayers $1,500 per autopsy because we don't have a medical examiner in Santa Cruz County. Every deceased body was transported to Tucson. Some years there were fifteen people found. That was a hit on our budget. In addition, because the whole immigration system is broken, the drug cartels began smuggling people. There was trouble, and our sheriffs had to respond to 911 calls or bring in the border patrol. All of this was a burden on the county.

I'm sorry to say that for many Americans, drugs and illegal immigrants have become inseparable. Given my life, that is not my view.

First, the drugs. The United States has 5 percent of the world's population. Yet tragically, we consume 50 percent of the drugs. This problem wasn't created by Mexico, and with that level of demand here, along with the size of our country and our importing goods by land, air, and sea, it's impossible to believe we can stop drugs from being brought in—unless we seal ourselves off from the world.

Do drug dealers south of our border take advantage of us? Absolutely. But the same thing can be said of drug dealers across the globe. Ask anyone on the border patrol or our county sheriff and they will tell you—drugs, not people, are the biggest law enforcement problem.

We have been fortunate. We haven't had too many surges of undocumented immigrants. Our sheriff and local police have developed a good working relationship with the border patrol. That is key to protecting our community and allowing us to make immigration here tolerable. The federal government has done an excellent job for us.

Yet, and I hate to say it, there is some hypocrisy in the resistance to immigration from Mexico. As citizens who live here, we encourage our children to go to college and do better economically. I haven't noticed long lines of Americans waiting to work in the fields. And why should they? It's backbreaking work for low wages.

I had a job as a produce inspector, so I've seen people work in the onion fields. I've been there when it is 115 degrees and they're sorting and packing onions or they're in that heat cutting broccoli stems and putting them in boxes to be shipped around the country.

The same is true in the construction trades. My sister used to work for AAA in Omaha, Nebraska, and she would insure a lot of these contractors. The contractors preferred to employ Mexicans. They would work Monday through Sunday. If the contractor needed them to work overtime, they worked overtime. And my sister told me this wasn't what the contractors found when they hired local guys. They'd pick up their first check, and the contractors would never see them again.

The reality is we need immigrants. Americans want their fruit and vegetables and dairy products. They want their houses built. But they don't want to do the labor. So who will?

I've seen these immigrants find their niche here. People who started out as dishwashers and now have their own businesses. They weren't interested in living off the public dime. They understood if you work hard, the opportunities will come for you to take care of your loved ones, to put food on the table, to see a doctor when you're sick, and the list goes on. It's more than simply owning a house with a white picket fence.

As I've watched these strivers, here's what I learned—my father wasn't the only one who taught his children to be responsible and to value hard work.

Another lesson my mother and father taught us was to make a difference in your community by being civic-minded. I've been in county government for over twenty-one years, and on our local school board for thirty. And while we can't solve the challenge of immigration reform locally, it's local government that has a far clearer picture of the challenges and rewards than our officials in Washington, D.C.

That's why I've been involved with the National Association of Counties (NACo) Immigration Reform Task Force for the last decade. These are local leaders who get to see the problem close up and hear stories like the family who lost their strawberry business because they couldn't find help to pick them. The H-2A temporary visas for agricultural workers have helped and we'd like to see that program expanded. Wouldn't it be smart for us to figure out how many people for agriculture, construction, and a whole range of work are needed and then permit that number to enter? Wouldn't it make sense if an employer finds good workers and wants to keep them, that they should be able to stay instead of being told, "Your three years are up, now go find work elsewhere?"

Unfortunately, when people hear us talk about immigration reform, all they hear is amnesty, and we're not pushing for amnesty. We're trying to find a reasonable path to citizenship. There are opportunities for people to earn their way, to follow the law, to earn legal status, and eventually have the chance to become an American citizen. This is the narrative we and others—for example, the chambers of commerce—have pushed and will continue to push, so hopefully we can find a happy medium and an answer to those politicians and Americans intent on vilifying everyone who wants to come across as drug dealers, rapists, or freeloaders.

In my line of work, you have to be an optimist. To find a real solution is going to take intestinal fortitude from our lawmakers, which is why the relationship that NACo and some of our federal partners have built must continue. Members of Congress and administrations change, but we need a constant presence of people who understand what's going on. It's not about what immigrants get when they arrive—it's about what they give back while they live here.

I could go on about the practical reasons for reasonable immigration policies, but for me, the moral aspect is equally important. Not long ago, a colleague phoned me and complained about all the children illegally crossing the border. I said, "Let me ask you this. How desperate does a parent have to be to entrust their child to complete strangers in hopes that they will get them over here? Are you suggesting that the children be sent back across the line so that some predator or somebody can take advantage of them?"

"No," he replied. "That's not what I'm suggesting."

And I told him, "Our first statement about who we are as a country claims that our rights have been granted by the Creator. So, if God is part of the national equation, then isn't it our responsibility to help those less fortunate?"

Not only that. I know from my parents' lives, and the lives of their eleven children, that this acceptance is also in our nation's best interest.

HUNGER

Commissioner Larry Johnson
DeKalb County, Georgia

"We have to look at hunger and its relationship to economics, wellness, and empowerment."

I'm the child of teenage parents from the South Side of Chicago. I was the first one in my family to attend college. In 1986, when I left for the University of Illinois Urbana-Champaign, there were more crack dealers than stores on the South Side, and about 500 or 600 homicides a year. I received my master's degree in public health from the University of Northern Colorado. It was there that I found my passion, connecting my life experience and education, and decided to work with struggling communities. After moving to Georgia, I was elected to the board of commissioners in DeKalb County in 2002.

The population of DeKalb County is just over three-quarters of a million with close to 16 percent of our people living in poverty. Yet food insecurity during the COVID-19 pandemic appeared to range across income brackets. When we had food drives and distributions, the line was a mile long and you saw everyday people. You know how we stereotype people based on the cars they drive? Well, there were all types of cars in line. Lower-income and middle-income folks were hungry. Before the pandemic, I organized a food drive every year. But the drive after COVID-19 hit was stunning. I had hundreds of volunteers and we gave out over twenty-four tons of food.

The pandemic ripped the band-aid off a lot of issues around food insecurity, but it has been on my mind for the last fifteen years. Some time ago, I created a place for residents to plant a garden in a public park and to access safe, clean water. But beyond whatever fixes that can be applied, we have to look at public policy. When we talk about food deserts, we focus on the noun, not the verb. The verb is how did they become deserted? Where is the economic development? Why do people in these areas have to travel twenty miles to a grocery store, which costs them more in gas and time? And if there is one grocery store in the neighborhood, it might be at the gas station. And you know what you get at a gas station? Not fresh fruits and vegetables. You get processed foods. We have to look at hunger and its relationship to economics, wellness, and empowerment.

KEY STATS

Fifty-three percent of counties have food insecurity rates above the national rate of 12.5 percent.

I've always tried to find the assets in a community and to partner with them. One of the key assets in any county is the Extension Services program, 4-H. I did it in Chicago, and people asked, "Why you got a 4-H program in an urban area?" Because we had a teacher, Miss Chew. No pun intended. She taught us how to grow Swiss chard. She gave us a little plastic bag with seeds, and we watched them grow and repotted them outside behind the school. I was fascinated by it. My granddad in Mississippi was a mini-farmer. He had his own garden in a vacant lot. Everybody was laughing about it until the collard greens, tomatoes, and cucumbers popped up. Then everybody was coming by to get what my granddad grew.

In Georgia, before I was elected a county commissioner, I ran a program, Reach for Wellness, which took a racial and ethnic approach to community health. It was the largest program in the state. I was connected to a great guy, Bobby Wilson, who was with 4-H. Bobby was phenomenal. We focused on healthy eating. We had gardens for employees who were leaving the county to go home where they could pick up fruits and vegetables. Later on, we sent a truck out into the county during the spring and summer for residents who wanted our freshly grown produce. We've been doing this for seven or eight years now. We don't just lecture people about healthy eating. We create easy avenues for them to make wise food choices.

I grew up on food stamps. The first week you got a lot of stuff because the stamps came in. But by the second or third week, you were eating potatoes and syrup sandwiches. Thank God for that commodity food—the peanut butter and powdered milk. Having been through that, I understand the situation from the inside out and how to reach people trying to make ends meet. We have more resources now—computers and email and websites—but there is still a lack of communication and collaboration around access to food. Being a county commissioner and past president of the National Association of Counties, I have local and national resources to help.

Nearly every county has poverty. The impoverished suffer from a lack of food and frequently other issues—whether it be living around high crime or mental-health problems. So the question for those who want to help is, "How do I connect the dots?" You have to take a multifaceted approach and collaborate with others. You can do surface-level stuff and throw money on the table, but that's not a long-term solution. You have to teach people how to advocate to bring grocery stores to their communities or form co-ops by teaming with farmers. Having those resources available to assist folks who want to take those extra steps is very important to me.

I sponsored legislation and the board passed an ordinance allowing groups to farm in a park. All they had to do was sign up for it. These park farms can create a healthy supply of food and build healthy communities and exercises among residents. In the wake of that success, I worked to create a garden and an orchard in a park along with the residents, who loved them. They ate fruit from the trees. The point here is not just the immediate results plus the additional benefits of community engagement, new collaborations, and strengthened partnerships. It's that I can showcase the achievements to nonprofits who want to help these communities. We've been fortunate that a number of them have signed on.

The Community Foundation has a program, the Neighborhood Fund, which hands out $500 grants for community innovation. The United Way supports community building. The Atlanta Food Bank is key in fighting food insecurity. They have the Hunger Walk. Hosea Helps supplies food. During Easter weekend, we host a food distribution in the county where we give out 5,000 bags of groceries. We also work with at least six churches. During the COVID-19 pandemic, we supplied over 100 tons of food. The churches become even more crucial as we head into May and June because the neediest children are not receiving their school breakfasts and lunches. If we could fund it, I would support opening up the schools during the summer vacation to feed children in the mornings and afternoons.

In the long run, we need a national agenda to combat poverty. That means finding ways to catch the attention of our elected officials in state capitals and Washington, D.C. There are many impactful local programs that could use more funding. I've asked Decide DeKalb, the economic development arm of the county, to consider financial incentives for bringing grocery stores to underserved communities. They don't have to be big-box stores. They can be smaller grocery chains that could use the infusion of capital or meaningful tax breaks.

I've also thought it would be beneficial for the U.S. Department of Agriculture and the Department of Housing and Urban Development to team up to create community gardens in housing developments. This isn't some fantasy of mine. I've seen it. A woman I met has been tending one of these gardens for thirty years and it's still going strong. I remember seeing her and she had a hat with the fruit and vegetables on it. She was a social worker, but she used her free time to grow food and her neighbors loved that garden. It was intergenerational. That's another part of confronting poverty: you need everyone involved—the young and the old seeking solutions.

Community is key. If you want policies to change, you have to advocate. Community members have to be at the center of all of these approaches. It's a message I carry everywhere: We are a government "of the people, by the people, for the people."

Don't ever give up the power you have to make change. Don't leave it to Larry Johnson. Don't leave it to President Biden. Don't leave it to Senators Ossoff and Warnock. You, the individual citizen, have that power, and you must use it to improve your life.

PUBLIC SAFETY

EMERGENCY RESPONSE

Commissioner Pamela Tokar-Ickes
Somerset County, Pennsylvania

"All of us, during this tragedy, were hands-on, yet none of us were emergency gurus. We simply divvied up the responsibilities."

My career on the board of commissioners was forged in the crucible of a national tragedy.

It was a bright, blue September morning. Our three-person board was speaking with a men's coffee group that got together monthly on Tuesdays at somebody's cabin in Friedens, a town a few miles from my house. We finished discussing our current projects and headed back to Somerset, the county seat, for our biweekly commissioner's meeting. We stopped at a diner for breakfast and as we paid our check, someone came out of the kitchen, saying, "A plane hit one of the towers of the World Trade Center."

A terrible accident, we thought, and drove to Somerset. At the time, our 911 center was in the basement of the courthouse and downstairs a TV was tuned to CNN. Onscreen, the tower was burning. Our 911 director said nothing had been determined yet. I walked across the street to our office building. We were looking over the agenda when our emergency management director informed us that a plane had gone down near Shanksville. I returned immediately to the 911 center.

My fellow commissioners, Brad Cober and Jimmy Marker, had our meeting during which they signed an emergency declaration, standard protocol following any disaster that allows you to access federal funding to offset the costs of cleaning up in the wake of the devastation.

All of the commissioners returned to the 911 center, where the director and others were fielding phone calls left and right. A second plane had hit the other tower of the World Trade Center and another plane had crashed into the west side of the Pentagon. Evidently, it was a terrorist attack, and it seemed the crash in Shanksville was involved. A team from the Pennsylvania Emergency Management Agency showed up and pulled the board members aside. They said, "The crash site in Shanksville is the county's financial responsibility from start to finish. Nobody's going to do this for you."

KEY STATS

Counties invest annually over $42 billion on over 3,000 police and sheriff departments.

I drove out to the site with the sheriff. Smoke was still rising from the wreckage and people in bio suits were working. By the time I returned to my office, my voicemail was filled with residents volunteering to help. Our coroner held the crash site for more than a year, and our sheriff's deputies patrolled it until finally the National Park Service took over and created the Flight 93 National Memorial.

I recount this story because it demonstrates why I'm so proud to serve on the board of a small rural county. All of us, during this tragedy, were hands-on, yet none of us were emergency gurus. We simply divvied up the responsibilities. One of my fellow commissioners worked closely with the coroner's office; another assisted with purchasing for what was needed for the recovery site; and I was tasked with putting together a memorial service that drew thousands to the steps of our courthouse.

Still, then and now, our biggest challenge is funding. We were reimbursed by the federal government for most of the money we spent, but that was a special case. Normally, for emergency services, we rely on volunteers, primarily our fire departments. One of our largest expenses is enabling our emergency services to communicate with each other. The police must talk to EMS who must talk to the fire departments. That required a multimillion dollar investment in technology. We are in the process of our second radio upgrade since 9/11. We are adding tower sites and upgrading the radios for all of our county emergency-service departments. Volunteer fire departments rely on fundraising events, but we couldn't expect our fire department to raise enough to cover the radios, so the county also paid for them.

We are also facing a problem that is impacting the entire nonprofit sector, a shortage of volunteers. It's hit volunteer fire departments very hard. The training requirements are stringent; the time commitment is heavy; and they literally place their lives on the line whenever they go out on a call. Rural counties are losing their younger populations. I think the average age for a volunteer fire department in Pennsylvania is 55, so sustaining these departments is difficult.

For instance, we have a team that goes to the scene of hazmat spills. With the Pennsylvania Turnpike and several other highways crisscrossing the county, there is a constant influx of hazardous materials passing through. We had a local fire department handling the hazmat calls, but they came to the board and said they couldn't recruit enough volunteers and could no longer handle it.

We straightened out that situation by cobbling together a county hazmat team, drawing our crew from a number of volunteer fire departments across Somerset County. That was an unusual and cost-savings arrangement because many counties dealt with it by contracting out to a third-party private company. But ten years ago, we declined that arrangement.

One challenge that weighs heavily on me is the possibility of an unforeseen emergency. With our population at about 72,000 and a budget of just under $50 million, it is nearly impossible to expand our pool of volunteers, and our budget is mostly allocated. This is why the COVID-19 pandemic hit our emergency services so hard.

We were extremely lucky that we did not have the number of fatalities they had in other parts of the country. But our emergency services folks also serve as 911 dispatchers. Many of them, when they weren't working for the county, were going on EMS runs and unfortunately a lot of them were personally affected by the virus.

The estimated costs of the pandemic were staggering. We wondered if people losing their jobs would be able to pay their property taxes, which account for over 50 percent of our revenue. Our jail required more funding to protect the staff and inmates from the virus. We had caseworkers and probation officers in the field, and we were paying overtime for our 911 dispatchers. Some county governments reduced their staff, but we chose not to in order to ensure that our employees were available to provide services to our residents. At the same time, we were concerned about the financial stability of their own families and health insurance at a moment when they may have needed those benefits the most. A big percentage of our costs were for personnel.

In the end, federal funding saved our budget, covering our costs, and the stimulus checks helped people pay their property taxes. Yet the experience underscored for me just how vulnerable our county—and all smaller counties are—to unpleasant surprises. Our board wanted to try to be ready for the next event. Beginning with 9/11 and through the COVID-19 pandemic, our discussions ramped up several levels about how we could avoid wasting resources by duplicating services that we could acquire elsewhere.

Fortunately, Somerset County became part of Pennsylvania's Region 13. It is a consortium of now fourteen counties. Region 13 sees itself as "a model for intergovernmental and multi-jurisdictional cooperation." The arrangement formalizes our working hand in hand with other counties— for example, setting up redundancies so if one county's 911 system goes down another county can pick up the dispatch responsibility. You can also access a variety of other services such as training and equipment for first responders.

The point is—and it is a critical one for smaller counties facing what we all suspect will be an economically demanding future—there is not only strength in numbers, but a significant increase in your abilities to provide services at a cost your taxpayers can bear.

This is the future I see, and a strategy I believe in.

911 SERVICES

Assistant County Manager Dakisha (DK) Wesley
Buncombe County, North Carolina

"Whatever someone's reason for dialing those three numbers, I always consider the person answering the call as the first, first responder."

Every county is different. You have to evaluate whether it's a good idea to consolidate your 911 services based on the needs and the trajectory of your specific county before moving in that direction. Most important—always put people first in that deliberation.

When I think about 911, I typically think of it as a resident, not as a government employee. Most people call 911 because they have a safety or medical crisis. Lately, we've found that a lot of the calls concern a mental-health crisis. Whatever someone's reason for dialing those three numbers, I always consider the person answering the call as the first, first responder. Usually, we see the police, the fire department, and the ambulance service as our first responders, and they are. But it all starts with the 911 dispatcher.

Do residents care who is responding? When there is a crisis, I doubt it. And it's important to remember this when you are discussing consolidating your emergency-call response. Our largest municipality is Asheville, but we have five others and when a person in distress phones, someone must arrive quickly. One of the things I've learned working in local government is oftentimes people you interact with don't think in terms of local versus state versus federal. We think about it because it is frequently tied to funding, but the people just know that it's the government, and they want the government to function effectively.

Buncombe County is growing significantly, and our call volume grew during the COVID-19 pandemic and will continue to grow after it's over. This is why it's crucial to make accurate projections about growth in order to ensure that our 911 center can meet the needs today and tomorrow. Also, dispatchers must be prepared to respond to different types of crises. One of the developments we're seeing in Buncombe County—and it is, I believe, a nationwide phenomenon—is an increase of medical or mental-health issues. That wasn't the case when I began working in local government twenty years ago. As the type of issues change, we have to be prepared to respond to those changes.

KEY STATS

Counties invest almost $107 billion in justice and public safety services.

To accomplish this, we have to make sure our dispatchers are healthy mentally and physically. We must provide them with the tools to deal with our residents when they're in very high distress, which means training on how to speak to people. The other thing that's important to us in Buncombe County is understanding that our population is quite diverse. Keeping in mind the cultural differences—and at times, language differences—when you interact with the folks calling into the 911 center is crucial.

Frequently, the dispatchers have to be very skilled, and I could never do their job. I don't have a hat on, but if I did, I'd tip it to them. They are not social workers, but they need to know how to speak to people as if they were. They need to provide information in a timely way to callers, and in a manner that people still feel safe and understand that they are speaking to someone who is going to respond and cares about them. The dispatchers then have to make sure they are communicating clearly to our medical folks and our police and fire departments—and not only the situation they are describing but also from a technology standpoint, and quickly with the appropriate protocol. Their work entails constant learning and they must multitask under pressure while appreciating the demands of communicating with diverse populations. This is a greater challenge in a consolidated system because residents, even in a single county, can be from a variety of subcultures, and the dispatchers must react to that in a matter of moments. They are, in my opinion, super men and women.

Our responsibility, as county officials overseeing 911 services, is to make certain that there are enough resources and tools for the dispatchers. Resource allocation is one of the hardest responsibilities from a county management perspective. We have a strategic plan, and our board has told us what they want from us moving forward. Of course, you need resources to move into the future, and some of what they want is visionary and long-term and expensive. We have to balance a strategic vision against our immediate priorities and meeting all of our legal mandates. To gauge how our 911 services are faring, we are fortunate to have no shortage of data. Our computers tell us the number of calls and the time it takes to dispatch. We know how many transfers we have to make. With all of this information to aggregate, we can present a good case to our board for providing additional resources.

The solution to the funding pinch is consolidating 911 services. In Buncombe County, we previously had not only the county dispatchers, but the city of Asheville and the town of Black Mountain had dispatchers as well. When I arrived here, for the most part, we were responding to calls from these three places. That meant when a call came in, we had to transfer it to the appropriate center. That takes time, and in a crisis—say, a heart attack—shaving a minute or two off the response can be the difference between life and death. By consolidating, by setting up one answering and dispatching point, you're not only saving money, but saving lives, too. Buncombe County just had three centers. In some counties in the United States, there can be multiples of our number.

Our consolidation played out over a period of three years, but the full-force earnest work lasted for about a year and a half. When I talk to people in other jurisdictions, they say, "That was fast! How in the world did y'all do that so fast?" I think if everybody knows the goal and pushes toward that goal in the same direction, you can get it done in a timely fashion. And it can be done without any huge up-front infrastructure costs.

There are other advantages. With all of our people under the same roof, it is easier to establish consistency in leadership and training so every resident gets the same high level of service. What's helpful for us is it allows us to have a space where we can innovate because we know the county's needs are changing and increasing. The COVID-19 pandemic, coming out of nowhere, it seemed, has shown just how much our responsibilities can change. From a decision-making standpoint, once we figure out the actions we want to take, we can disseminate that information to our staff.

We're looking at the data to see the types of response codes that we have. Some of the things that we traditionally would be responding to—are they at the level of criminality or potential criminality where it needs to be a police officer? Or should it be someone who is a community paramedic or community worker that's responding? That's how we are changing— reimagining how we respond to instances where people are in crisis.

We, as county officials, understand how critical 911 is to the quality of life here and we strive to make sure the center is the best that it can be now and in the future. We are looking at the concept of stationing medical personnel in the 911 center who could possibly co-respond to a caller along with a dispatch person. Perhaps a nurse who can resolve issues that might not necessarily require someone going to a site. Some of those things can be worked out as a part of the 911 center. We're looking at that around the county, making sure we're aligning with best practices, because if there is one thing my experience in government has taught me, it is that reinventing the wheel is a waste of time and money.

JAILS

Commissioner Janet Thompson
Boone County, Missouri

"Mental illness will always be with us. There will always be more to do."

I'd completed a master's degree in Spanish at the University of Missouri and was en route to a Ph.D. before I realized that I was unlikely to land a job teaching Golden Age Spanish poetry. So off I went to law school, and when I was hired as a public defender, I was happy to discover my Spanish wasn't wasted. Missouri has a substantial Hispanic population and, like most state public-defender systems, we were chronically underfunded. When one of my colleagues needed to talk to a witness or client who was a Spanish speaker or had limited English, I was lassoed to go along for the interview.

After twenty-five years as an assistant public defender, I entered politics believing I could do more to help my community in office. In 2012, I was elected Boone County District II (Northern) Commissioner, re-elected in 2016 and again in 2020.

For a quarter-century, I had defended clients with considerable mental health issues. I have a good friend who works in the field, and she likes to say that mental illness is the only non-casserole disease, meaning that whenever anyone gets sick, you bring them a casserole. Except if they live with mental illness. In addition, the problems I saw in mentally ill defendants were frequently complicated by drug addiction—the drug use often the result of these troubled souls attempting to cope with their demons. The worst place for these people was jail, and yet judges sent them there. A tragic miscarriage of justice, in my view, and not in the best interest of society. As a public defender, I fought it on a case-by-case basis until I felt as overwhelmed as the so-called "Little Dutch Boy" trying to plug a dike with his finger.

KEY STATS

The cost of correctional facilities for counties has reached $29 billion.

Then, during a meeting, I heard folks at the National Association of Counties (NACo) talking about their Stepping Up Initiative, a program that brought together the Council of State Governments Justice Center and the American Psychiatric Association Foundation to advocate for counties hoping to keep individuals with mental illness and substance-use issues out of jail when possible. This was precisely the course I wanted to pursue. However, we lacked data on the number of these inmates in our jail, how long they stayed and, most important, their recidivism rates. Someone on my team suggested the county undertake a study and asked if I'd ever heard of one.

No, I hadn't, but I wanted to find out if one existed—there is no bigger waste of time and money than reinventing the wheel. I phoned Nastassia Walsh, the director of programs and operations for the Counties Futures Lab at NACo, and we discussed the idea. I told her we wanted to identify every single person in the county jail who had mental-health challenges. They could have been identified by a defense counsel, prosecutor, judge, detention staff, mental-health professional, or even a family member. Once identified, we wanted to bring them to a group for evaluation every two weeks. Our goal was to eliminate situations where people were sitting in jail who shouldn't be there or who shouldn't have been charged in the first place and instead diverted to treatment.

I was told that Johnson County, Iowa, was exploring the issue, and we latched onto their approach. (My motto is, as songwriter and mathematician Tom Lehrer said, "Plagiarize, plagiarize, that's why

God made your eyes.") As we began to collect data, we discovered that detainees with mental health problems returned to jail at a far higher rate than detainees without those challenges. Not only that, they were in jail longer than other detainees facing similar circumstances. We wanted to know the reason. No one here had explored that before, and it was easy for anybody familiar with county jails to understand why: the jails are overcrowded, and the staff is overworked, so asking employees to do one more thing when a detainee arrives is tough.

We charged on without much funding and with the cooperation of our people. We stole a short-form mental-health assessment from somewhere—honestly, I can't remember from where—and began to get a handle on our detainees' issues. The thing that has probably had the greatest impact—and again, we stole this one from Johnson County— was that we took a hard look at the length of time inmates were spending in the county jail and asked ourselves why they were locked up for so long.

Because of Stepping Up, we now have staffing to deal with the mentally ill in our jail. We have a mental-health professional and trained detention staff. We also have people looking at whether a person should actually be incarcerated. We have someone from the prosecutor's office and the public defender. If an inmate is represented by private counsel, private counsel comes in. Our diversion court commissioner checks to see if an inmate can be diverted. We have a judge who doesn't hear criminal cases so she doesn't have to recuse herself when reviewing a detainee's case.

Leslie Schneider is the judge, and I'll never forget the day she called out the prosecutor, saying, "Why is this person in our county jail? This is ridiculous. This person does not need to be here."

Once we reached that conclusion, everyone started brainstorming about the resources we could provide to get this person into a better situation because he was decompensating in jail. Could we find supportive housing? Behavioral health intervention? Transportation? Job training? All of those factors to get him out of jail and to keep him out.

Recently, we've had some bitter cold weather and a gentleman has been coming into our building to warm up. Most of the time, he is clearly in the midst of a mental-health crisis and he may also have intellectual disabilities. He's a large man but very vulnerable to folks on the street because he is so meek and mild, and people take his hat and coat and gloves and steal what little money he has. Still, a few years ago, some of his annoying behavior in our building would have landed him in the county jail. But now, our team recognizes his problems and helps him. Which is how it should be. Being annoying in public doesn't mean you belong in a cell.

As proud as I am of the headway we've made, the true and sometimes unappreciated beauty of NACo's Stepping Up is not only that it has provided another lens through which to view the justice system and changed our approach to the mentally ill; it has also changed minds.

Initially, the sheriff was hesitant to adopt our approach—in part, I believe, because I was a public defender and he considered me concerned with criminals at the expense of victims. Yet after seeing the program in action, he came onboard and became an advocate and lives our message. All of his deputies and detention staff receive forty hours of training by a Crisis Intervention Team. It certainly doesn't give them a master's degree in social work, but it does sensitize them to mental-health issues and teaches how to de-escalate potentially violent confrontations.

This program has shown success, and we were able to do it on a shoestring budget, but we still have to figure out housing—a huge problem made worse by the COVID-19 pandemic. If you divert individuals from the justice system and they don't have a place to go, odds are good they will end up back in a jail cell.

One of the crucial lessons I learned from my involvement with the Justice and Public Safety Committee at NACo was the importance of building regional alliances and the Missouri Association of Counties started a Policing, Justice and Mental Health Steering Committee, which has helped us create better ways of communicating and working together across our region. We have public administrators and sheriffs involved in the process. If you have more stakeholders at the table then you can ask, "Gosh, what motivated that decision? What motivated that policy?" You can start asking those questions in a non-accusatory way and begin to evaluate your decision-making at every single level and perhaps keep more people out of the criminal-justice system.

We have accomplished a great deal, but there is far more to do. I'd like to see a regional 24/7 center that can be contacted to deal with any situation that arises. I'd like to see us start interceding earlier with the mentally ill, when they first need help, before they wind up standing in a courtroom.

I suppose my feelings are a natural result of the progress we've made. But I want to do more. Because mental illness will always be with us, there will always be more to do.

HUMAN TRAFFICKING

District Attorney Nancy O'Malley
Alameda County, California

"We all need to remember: It can happen anywhere."

When I was growing up, I used to go to work with my dad. He was the District Attorney of Contra Costa County. He funded the first rape crisis center in the county and probably the second in California. Eventually, I volunteered as a rape-crisis advocate in 1975. I learned so much when I joined the Alameda County District Attorney's Office as a deputy district attorney in 1984. I was one of the few lawyers who had dealt with sexual-assault victims. No one was using the term "human trafficking."

Then, in 1997, I had a case—a twelve-year-old girl raped by a fifty-year-old man in a motel room. She lived in Oakland with her single mom and two sisters. Sitting with the girl at her mom's house, I conducted one of the saddest interviews I'd ever done. I can still picture myself trying to make eye contact with this shy little girl. I asked her, "Do you feel like you're safe on the street?" and she said, "That's where I'm the most safe," because the thirty-nine-year-old man selling her for sex watched over her. The man caught with her in the motel—he was the seventh man she'd been sold to that night.

I prosecuted one man as a rapist, the other as a facilitator of rape, and I began to speak publicly about it. I referred to the girls as "sexually exploited minors," but when I attempted to explain to people what that meant, it fell on deaf ears, as if they couldn't imagine American kids were being sold for sex. In 2003, a colleague and I wrote a bill to create the crime of human trafficking in California, and it was carried by a legislator from Orange County. He even recounted a story to other legislators about a golf tournament in the county where trailers were set up off one of the fairways, beyond the trees. Girls were brought in, and some of the golfers and spectators went into the trailers and paid for sex. It wasn't run-of-the-mill prostitution because many of the girls were minors. Still, the legislator couldn't even get our bill out of committee.

KEY STATS

Counties bring together law enforcement, social service agencies and other county organizations to address human trafficking.

A year later, there was a stronger movement and legislation was passed in Sacramento. However, it was only what the federal government defined as trafficking, and it gave prosecutors no teeth. At the same time, I was putting on statewide conferences; I called them, "All Things Teen." The first year I did a presentation on human trafficking and five people showed up. The second year, about fifty people came. The third year, I had to open the walls of two conference rooms to accommodate the law enforcement people, victim advocates, and prosecutors. And I made this point: what people called "teen prostitution" was actually human trafficking.

In general, people resisted embracing the concept and continued blaming the victim. We began showing photographs of young girls being dressed up like adult sex workers or being physically abused, including being burned because they refused to go out on the street. We adopted a saying: "Not every child will be trafficked, but every child is vulnerable to being trafficked."

By now, I was chief assistant DA, and I realized we needed a broader strategy and action plan. In 2005, the Alameda County District Attorney's Office began its five-pronged model program to fight human exploitation and trafficking, called H.E.A.T. Watch.

First, we had to prosecute these cases, which is a key component of the initiative. If a trafficker was sentenced to prison, that would serve as a deterrent to others. I created a specialized unit to prosecute human traffickers and increased the number of victim advocates. We had eight or ten; now we have almost fifty.

Second, we had to train police who were arresting the girls. The girls wound up in juvenile hall as offenders. We changed that practice. And we spent a lot of time interviewing these young women to educate their lawyers about trafficking. Again, our motto was "there's no such thing as a child prostitute!"

Third, those interviews convinced me that we also needed nongovernment advocacy. Many of the girls had been brainwashed into distrusting the police when in fact, the whole legal system was supposed to protect them. Yet they were psychologically bonded to their traffickers, very much like Stockholm syndrome; they believed the traffickers had to be shielded from law enforcement. This made the young women reluctant to testify against the trafficker in court. We encouraged and partnered with community-based organizations to form and to focus on human trafficking.

Fourth, we took on the law. Neither the federal nor state statutes were clearly defined, and part of my advocacy became traveling to the Capitol in Sacramento and educating the legislators about the criminal enterprise at the core of which was exploiting and harming children. They knew me because I'd been up there for other bills regarding interpersonal violence, and once again, I became a broken record for the cause. I started flying to Washington, D.C., and talking to policymakers. I recall one Congress member saying to me, "I really don't know what you mean. Explain it to me." I was one voice among many. The Polaris Project, which fights sex and labor trafficking around the world, was a huge voice in Washington.

Fifth, we needed to educate the community. All of us understood that without public support, we would never change the faulty paradigm. So much of what we did was simply talk about human trafficking everywhere we could. The more we talked, the more people—at least in Alameda County—became sensitized to it. Soon, other counties and the state were listening, too. Our success in educating the community was enhanced by our sharing of the H.E.A.T. Watch Blueprint. This also helped other communities create their own initiatives to effectively combat trafficking—not only in California, but across the country.

The sad truth was that people just weren't getting it, and I would speak in other states, hand out our materials and encourage them to confront the problem. I certainly wasn't the only one. The National Association of Counties, with its ability to impact local government, was also involved for years spreading the word—whether it was gangs trafficking women or the fate of victims or the programs that existed to address the problem.

Finally, in 2012, we were able to get our initiative, Proposition 35, on the ballot. In California, voters can vote in a law and if it passes, the legislature can't undermine it by changing the law. That is the bad and the good news. If you get it wrong, you're stuck with it. If you get it right, you can make real, positive changes.

Proposition 35 raised the maximum penalty for human trafficking from eight years to fifteen-years-to-life and levied fines of up to $1.5 million. In addition, the proposition mandated that anyone convicted of human trafficking had to register as a sex offender and would have to disclose any activity in cyberspace. Proposition 35 enhanced other legislation and policies in place. For instance, law enforcement would have to be trained how to recognize and to stop human trafficking. And if a case made it to court, the defense lawyer couldn't impeach the victim by introducing evidence of prior sexual behavior.

Proposition 35 received over 10 million votes. That's more votes, I believe, than any other initiative in the history of California. It was approved by over 81 percent of voters. Now, ten years later, there is still a lot of work to do. We want the law to include and define human trafficking as a violent and serious felony. We need to devise therapeutic models for someone who has been trafficked. We have to look at the co-location of services and stop forcing victims to go to different places for help. In Alameda County, our Family Justice Center includes a "SPA" which is a Safe Place Alternative for trafficked girls. We need all of California to obey the law which mandates that every fifth, seventh, ninth, and eleventh grader be educated about human trafficking. San Diego has a great program and in Alameda County, we contract with 3Strands, an anti-human trafficking organization, to provide that education in every public school.

I could go on at length identifying innovative and effective approaches and programs, but most important is continuing to inform the public—today, tomorrow and forever more. We engage in a billboard campaign every January for Human Trafficking Awareness month. Our billboards are seen by 40 million sets of eyes each year. One cannot be driving in the Bay Area without knowing about it.

Yet, whenever you see a girl on the street soliciting, your gut reaction is to look away. When I talk to people about it, they'll say, "That's so sad. It happens in Oakland." And I say, "No, it happens in your community, too." The truth is it happens wherever there are young girls and young women and disrupted families and runaways and drugs and domestic violence—wherever there are all the troubles that we see in our communities.

Yes, we all need to remember: It can happen anywhere.

THE ENVIRONMENT AND LAND USE

ENVIRONMENTAL PRESERVATION

Supervisor Robert Weygandt
Placer County, California

"I discovered that I liked being in the thick of conservation efforts and it was a way to give back to a community that had been so good to my family and me."

In 1961, when I turned ten, my parents left the sprawl of Southern California and moved to the foothills of Placer County, a sparsely populated rural area in the northeastern part of the state. We lived on a small farm and my brother and sister and I were involved in 4-H programs. I loved the outdoors; I became a serious fly fisherman, though for college I enrolled at the University of Southern California, earning bachelor's and master's degrees in finance and management. I enjoyed my years in Los Angeles, but I felt the same pull that my parents had felt and I returned to Placer County to work for WECO Aerospace Systems, an aircraft repair facility that my dad and brother started. I rose to vice president, chief financial officer, and part owner of the company. After leaving there, I became a financial advisor.

My family and I were living on the farm where I grew up, but the county was experiencing explosive growth. Some people hated it; some people thought it was fine; and of course, as I was running for the board of supervisors, there was a lot of politicking around the issue.

I was elected to a seat, becoming one of five supervisors, and I've served on the board since 1995. Regarding growth, I was guided by core principles that I laid out to my colleagues. First, I didn't want the county to turn into Southern California. I wanted an approach that balanced the need for jobs and development with open space and environmental concerns. In 1997, two new supervisors were elected and our board organized a retreat. We had an all-day discussion that covered what kinds of open-space preservation policies would be acceptable to all of us and what were not acceptable. Staff members brought in research about programs that did a good job of managing growth. An important result of the retreat was reaching consensus to appoint a Citizen's Advisory Committee, whose members would be part of our dialogue with the state and federal environmental regulatory agencies.

KEY STATS

As of 2018, 184 counties in 22 states have been designated by the Environmental Protection Agency as not meeting 2015 standards for ground-level ozone.

This was setting a high bar. Many committed stakeholders worked for more than two years to produce the first comprehensive development blueprint, Placer Legacy, adopted in 2000. What it did was put the county in the business of considering and funding acquisitions of properties that we thought should be preserved as open space in perpetuity.

We put money behind our vision and invested a couple million dollars on scientific research and data collection so that we had a baseline of facts regarding habitat types. One major factor was development that destroyed vernal pools throughout the Sacramento Valley floor. Vernal pools are seasonal wetlands and form a unique ecosystem that provides habitat for numerous plants, insects, amphibians, and all manner of aquatic life. Many of the species are listed as protected or endangered and, in many cases, federal and state agencies have jurisdiction.

Politically, growth versus no growth was a divisive issue. Frankly, it took a while for the board to bite the bullet and make the tough decisions. It was an accomplishment that we were able to keep the effort alive through election cycles and new people joining and other people leaving the board.

We needed to draw a map that had the attributes for conservation and environmental protection. The particulars were arguable, but most of us knew we had to push back against developers and say, "We're going to do this. We can do it in a way that includes you as stakeholders, but you won't get everything you want."

I had one developer consultant tell me that they were designing a big project and the set-aside areas were going to look horrible, be filled with mosquitoes, and the residents would complain.

I said, "It strikes me that if you planned those well, you can actually make those open space properties an amenity. Put trails beside them, and people will actually like them."

Over the course of a decade, we made land acquisitions that became networks of trails and low-impact parklands open to the public. It will be a large task to knit together more than 47,000 acres of an interconnected reserve system (out of more than 260,000 acres of western Placer County) that our board of supervisors created to provide more protections for fish and wildlife.

Our board was extremely proud to adopt one of the first habitat conservation plans in the country. It integrated endangered species and aquatic resource permitting and conservation into our locally managed process. It has become a cliché, but this was a win-win outcome. The comprehensive plan adopted in 2020 was the culmination of untold hours of planning sessions and public meetings with stakeholders. We engaged in heated debates, but always respectfully, with the full spectrum of constituents committed to a prosperous Placer County that balances development and conservation. We feel we have established a lasting legacy by creating a model other counties can use.

One of the major benefits was cutting through red tape by enabling local entities rather than federal and state agencies to extend permit coverage to projects. It created a plan for property owners and project sponsors required to mitigate impacts on species and habitats. The plan offered alternatives to developers, who could either dedicate land to the reserve system or pay fees to support free-market easement or property acquisitions. It is a complex arrangement that achieves a tangible outcome: preservation of over 50 percent of the county's remaining stock of vernal pools.

Whenever possible, I tried to take politics out of the equation and was committed to making difficult decisions, whether I'd be re-elected or not. I also realized early on that the only way forward was through compromise. The bottom line to our success is that we forged friendships and developed relationships of trust along the way. I am proud of a 1,000-acre ranch the county purchased and transformed into a regional park with hikers, horseback riders, mountain bikers, and picnickers coexisting and utilizing thirty-five miles of trails. It is very popular and heavily used by our residents.

I am hopeful about the future for my two children, who both live and work in the area, and my four granddaughters and four grandsons. I like to take my grandchildren on hikes. Students from local schools spend hours poking around the edges of vernal pools and observing the magic below the placid surface of the water. They never tire of watching salamanders, frogs, and other aquatic wildlife. I feel confident that I had a hand in preserving that legacy for them and for generations to come. I also have witnessed the relentless pace of progress. It is unmistakable. When I moved back to Placer County permanently after college in 1980, the population was 3,200. Today, it's more than 50,000 and climbing. Despite the growth, we managed to preserve habitat for burrowing owls and salmon and steelhead trout still run in our streams.

When I was first elected to the county board, I thought I might serve one or two terms. I discovered that I liked being in the thick of conservation efforts and it was a way to give back to a community that had been so good to my family and me. I look forward to retirement after my term expires on December 31, 2022. I stood on the shoulders of some tremendous people, stewards of Placer County—most especially my parents, who found their slice of paradise far from Los Angeles. So many of us worked to preserve it, and we have left the work in good hands. I leave public service with no regrets. It has been a privilege.

CLIMATE PREPAREDNESS

Supervisor Connie Rockco
Harrison County, Mississippi

"Unless we change people's minds about what they're doing, unless we get them to buy in and understand the value of the resources that we have, I just think the situation here will erode."

When Hurricane Katrina struck New Orleans and the Mississippi Gulf Coast in late August 2005, I lived along the Tchoutacabouffa River, where I have lived since the early 1990s—just eleven feet above sea level. I've survived several floods and hurricanes during those decades, but Katrina was more powerful than anything anyone had imagined—a Category 5 hurricane with winds up to 175 mph and over 400 miles wide. It was the third-strongest hurricane ever recorded in the United States. It whipped up a twenty-foot-high storm surge. The death toll was 1,836 and another 705 people are still reported missing. The property damage and economic loss was a staggering $150 billion and 90,000 square miles were impacted by the floodwaters.

As a member of the board of supervisors, our duties include emergency management during a disaster such as a hurricane crisis. We set up our command center in the Civil Defense Department and I spent more than two weeks hunkered down there, meeting with county officials and emergency personnel every thirty minutes as we worked around-the-clock to assist with rescue and evacuation efforts. We take our duties and responsibilities to our people very seriously, placing ourselves last—much like soldiers, for example. I was afraid that my home had been washed away, and I couldn't summon the courage nor the time to look after experiencing the needs of others so hard hit.

Miraculously, my house survived. Only the roof was gone and ground floor flooded. The river crested well above its banks and did considerable damage to my home, but the floodwaters did not reach the upstairs floors. I felt very fortunate; so many others throughout the county were not so lucky. We are home to the country's last remaining unimpeded river, the Mississippi.

It is a unique environment, with the flow of fresh water from the river meeting the salt water of the Gulf of Mexico. It is not surprising, then, that we were once considered the seafood capital of the world with one of the world's largest shrimping industries, centered in Biloxi, and a large oyster industry as well. Overharvesting and the importing of seafood has sent those industries into decline.

Furthermore, we are in a very low area. We are the drainage basin of the entire state, so anything that happens upstream impacts us—not only the opening of the locks but also the cutting of trees, construction, and pollution running down from the floods. We are surrounded by water and we love it. That's why people are migrating here. Our population has hit 208,000. We have five cities. Trying to get those cities on the same page when they want to make sure that their tax dollars are secured by commercial building is a heavy lift. When you have construction, your water runs faster and developers are pushing to get things done. I wind up butting heads with many of them.

Our county is defined by water, by its beautiful bays, rivers, creeks, swamps, marshes, and the beaches, islands, and shores that connect it. This rich ecosystem creates unmatched habitats for an extraordinarily diverse and extensive number of flora and fauna species. It is also an especially fragile environment and the growing intensity of storms underscores the vulnerability of the Mississippi Gulf Coast due to climate change. It is an immense challenge to take concrete steps to plan for climate preparedness in an effort to mitigate the damage and impact of extreme weather and to create a more sustainable future.

We can pass laws, but unless we change people's minds about what they're doing, unless we get them to buy in and understand the value of the resources that we have, I just think the situation here will erode. The message I use is that for every dollar we spend on preventing flooding in advance saves the county taxpayer the six dollars we would have to spend to clean up after floods and to repair damage. That practical economics lesson resonates with our residents. Katrina was a destructive wakeup call and a spur to move much more quickly. We have heeded the warning and made some major improvements, including strengthening our building codes. New construction must build higher above the floodplain than in the past, based on frequently updated floodplain maps. We now require new homes to have three feet of freeboard where water can flow under the house without causing major water damage.

There have been some other recent bright spots. I have always been a strong advocate for renewable energy, reducing consumption, and recycling. I cheered when Coast Electric installed a large solar panel field. I have also been an active proponent to plant new trees as a way to help the environment and to honor deceased loved ones. I support strict oversight and stewardship of the 44,000 acres of national forest land in our county. I have urged tougher restrictions and stronger safeguards for our fragile wetlands and I don't think we have done enough to protect that tremendous asset that provides food and habitat for fish and wildlife, improves water quality, diminishes shoreline erosion, and serves as a floodwater storage basin. Since 1973, I have been a sad witness to the loss and degradation of our wetlands over the decades and I think they are often taken for granted. That's a mistake we need to rectify.

I had a front-row seat to observe the lack of coordination and breakdown of communication between county, state, and federal agencies after an environmental disaster like Hurricane Katrina or the Deepwater

Horizon oil rig spill in April 2010. It killed or severely harmed 82,000 birds, more than 6,000 sea turtles, and 25,000 marine mammals. It caused widespread shoreline damage and was the largest marine oil spill in history. Tourism, our life's blood, was also negatively affected as well as our seafood industries. I was on the response team when a group of people from Washington, D.C., came down to offer assistance. In my opinion, they did not really understand the situation and I saw many poor choices made during the cleanup. Counties have no voice at the table when the feds take over. Major decisions are made without the input of local and county government. We have the boots-on-the-ground knowledge and expertise, but it is rarely solicited—a major error from my perspective.

One of the fundamental problems I see is lack of communication across the numerous silos of government agencies. For example, the Corps of Engineers along the Mississippi River does not communicate well with its separate Corps in each state and district. Since Harrison County is at the bottom of the Mississippi watershed, we are impacted by manmade changes in dam lock opening and of freshwater releases, construction in drainage areas, and runoff from fertilizers and contaminants. Whatever flows into the Gulf of Mexico's Mississippi Sound can end up being a problem for Harrison County.

I have lived on the Mississippi Gulf Coast for one-half century and I have noticed a decline in water clarity, the fisheries, and the overall health of Mississippi Sound. I am embarrassed to admit that my husband and I travel to Alabama to fish because we have fewer concerns about contaminants and pollutants impacting the catch.

I don't want to leave the impression that the prognosis is all doom and gloom. We have the best seafood in the world. Our fishing and seafood industry is thriving despite our setbacks. We are resilient and will continue work on the conservation of our Gulf region. We have taken important first steps in reversing the decline and preparing for the effects of climate change and accelerating instances of extreme weather. I have recommended funding a study on the effects of increased storm water runoff. I have noticed that some businesses along the river have filled in sediment ponds and use the river as a kind of drainage ditch. This increases erosion and the possibility of contaminants being carried into the river. I want to fund research that documents this problem and then we can pass legislation to stop it before too much damage is done.

My husband is an engineer. He sees these problems as fixable and reversible, if we have the political will and commit resources for climate preparedness. For me, the number one issues are communication and education. Some will not hear what you have to say. Maybe they are turned off by the subject of climate change or it's just a matter of general indifference. It breaks my heart when I go to the beach and see litter on the sand. That doesn't happen too often, but why should it happen at all? Litter is so easy to control. I always wonder how people can toss stuff on public land. I don't understand it. I guess they figure someone else will pick up after them, and we do. But we need to educate people on that subject of trash disposal and recycling. I used to be a Keep America Beautiful girl. I suppose I still am.

The good news is that in the aftermath of Hurricane Katrina, departments across the county are communicating better. We all attend conferences sharing best practices on hurricane preparedness. We must continue to keep our focus on education and raising awareness. For me, after six terms on the board of supervisors, the bottom line is communication. We need to continue to talk about the new codes created in the wake of Katrina, and we need to underscore the fact that they are not just words on paper. They are the law and we will enforce them and punish violators. Our county's future, perhaps our very survival, depends on that.

WATER PRESERVATION

Commissioner Luis Sanchez
Midland County, Texas

"Our challenge is to have everything available to accommodate the influx of workers and their families, especially water."

Ever since I became a commissioner in 2009, our supply of potable water has been an issue. Over the last few years, it's gone from maybe the top five to our number one priority. We have aquifers down here, underground water sources that recharge. However, they recharge so slowly you can't depend on that water. I think the Ogallala and the Edwards Aquifers meet under us somewhere, but we can't really tap into those aquifers because they are too deep. Even if we did, the recharge is inadequate and it wouldn't be worth spending all that money. We have to look elsewhere, which is why we're trying to pipe in water.

The city of Midland is one of the fastest growing cities in the country. The residents inside the city limits receive their water through the city lines, but in the rural areas of the county, there are no water lines. All they have out there are wells and a lot of the wells have run dry. Some of the wells have been contaminated. We are in the Permian Basin with its hundreds of oil fields, and there is a good deal of drilling here. Due to the drilling, some of the companies have tainted some of the water with different types of pollutants, while other companies are actually out there attempting to clean the water so the residents can use it.

One way to deal with this problem is to increase our water supply. That was why we allocated $4.3 million to purchase the water rights of the Roark Ranch in Winkler County, which is two county lines over from us. That water is very good quality, requiring little to clean it. Our goal is to transfer the water here as soon as we can. We're hoping to pump about 2,000 gallons per minute, but we are still figuring out how to get it out there and how much it will cost the county and our residents. The price will be high because the county has far fewer residents than the city of Midland.

KEY STATS

Counties invest $22.6 billion in sewage and solid waste management annually.

Midland also bought a ranch, the T-Bar, and they built a $600 million pipeline to bring the water to Midland residents. We're trying to work with the city to come up with a way to transfer some of that water to the rural parts of the county, so they don't have to use their wells. We have some funding from different pockets—an infrastructure bill and state grants. We're tapping those resources and hoping to execute a trade with the city and start building the infrastructure.

Meantime, the conflict between Russia and Ukraine has sent the price of oil skyrocketing. And as soon as oil goes up, there are more jobs in the industry and more people coming out to Midland. Our challenge is to have everything available to accommodate the influx of workers and their families, especially water. We are trying to arrange to pipe it in from different places in West Texas. Because on top of everything else, the drought has been terrible. It broke for a few months, but now it's back again, and I think it's going to be with us for a long while. On top of the growth and that people can't use tainted water wells, we have a drought to worry about. We don't want water to be the reason people don't move to Midland County.

With the increase in families, developers will start building subdivisions. At first, the developers will drill wells, but we know that's not a permanent fix for the home buyers—the well water won't last. We are changing our strategy on how we move forward with residential and commercial real estate. The growth is massive. There's no more room in the city, so everybody's moving out into the county. We're building roads left and right as well. We finished our southern loop. Now that we've opened it, businesses are heading out to a rural area that has never been developed and has no water. People are anxious to build there, but they can't just build wherever they want. Oil comes first, then housing. Oil is the bloodline of this county, but water is essential for sustaining life. Still, it's more important for us to build oil wells. I don't say that as a bad thing; I see that as a great thing. But then you start wondering: how can we build a neighborhood around these wells?

I think many of our oil companies are making a great effort, but they're stuck if there's not enough water. With fracking, they're trying to come up with creative ways. Right now, they're buying the wastewater from the city of Midland, recycling it, and using that water for their drilling. That way, they're not using the clean water. They are also trucking in water from other areas. It could be they're buying it from other cities or water districts, but the point is their focus is on water—a focus we share.

The area that I represent south of Midland has been declared a *colonia* by the state of Texas. *Colonias* are impoverished communities where residents lack basic services—notably drinking water and sewage plants. They are a sad fact of life in Texas. There are over 2,000 of them with about half a million people. If your county is 150 miles from the Mexican border, you are eligible for a grant, so I applied for one and received it. With the funds we were able to bring in fifty septic tanks for low-income families.

An added benefit to the area's designation as a *colonia* is that we can tap into larger grants and loans which can finance the construction of water towers and pipelines. A key requirement to receiving those funds is that you must identify a water source and report it to the state. Because it would cost another $600 million to get that Roark Ranch water to the county, we are working to put together a deal with the city—for every gallon of water that the city can pump out at the Roark

Ranch, we get it back on the end in the county so we can distribute it to our residents.

We are still in the middle of negotiations, but the pipeline for the city of Midland is complete, and we're already getting water from there. It's a forty-eight-inch water transmission line that runs for about sixty miles—from Winkler County to Midland County. We're planning to construct another pipeline to connect the county with the city and use some of that water.

We are making progress. In the last primary election, the topic of water shot straight to the top. It was the talk of the town, and I don't ever remember people talking about it as frequently as they do now. My job, along with a colleague, is negotiating with the city, and we are in the midst of working on the details, talking to attorneys and engineering groups and political leaders, trying to find the best solution for both Midland County and the city of Midland. It's imperative out here in West Texas that we work with each other to come up with that solution because everybody in this area is trying to buy water rights. It's going to be a big fight, and the smart move is to start investing as much money as you can in locking up your water rights.

Even if we are successful and do achieve water security, our insecurity will be with us for the foreseeable future. It may not be our number one priority, but it won't fall too far down the list because we will always have to make sure that we pipe the water out to other residents in the county. That is going to be very expensive and it's going to take a lot of time. And once you reach that goal, you have to see to it that the water is clean when it comes out of the spigot in someone's home.

PUBLIC LANDS

Commissioner Joel Bousman
Sublette County, Wyoming

"The only way you develop the level of trust required is by working closely with people, making decisions with them by looking at the same piece of ground together, and then fixing the problem as best you can."

I'm a fourth-generation rancher and I've lived in Sublette County all of my seventy-three years.

Out here, the biggest problems counties face are financial and effectively communicating with the federal agencies that make public-lands decisions—mainly, in our case, the Bureau of Land Management and the U.S. Forest Service. We have to make sure they understand the customs and culture of the local counties and the economic base, and consider all of that when they make decisions.

The financial piece of it—and I'll use my county as an example—is that only 20 percent of our land is private and taxable. The rest belongs to the public. Our oil and natural gas revenues account for most of our budget, but with such a limited tax base, it's impossible for us to cover the costs of the services we have to provide: roads, law enforcement, search and rescue, and many others, without multiple use of our public lands. That's why the federal program, Payment in Lieu of Taxes (PILT), is critical to our local governments. On average, the amount of the dollars provided by PILT is not anywhere near to what those dollars would be if counties could tax that land as if it was owned privately, but we would be in a lot worse shape without it.

Yet while the PILT program is permanently authorized by Congress, it's not permanently funded. Every year, county commissioners from across the United States fly to Washington, D.C., and lobby. We meet with congressional staff and Congress people telling them why it's important they continue to fund the program and showing them how we use the money. For now, we've been successful. Our preference would be to have it funded so it becomes an annual obligation. That way, county governments could count on that money as part of their budget and be able to plan based on real revenue, not on what Congress decides to appropriate. But we haven't reached that point, which is why we have the National Association of Counties (NACo) fighting for us. We spend a lot of resources lobbying to keep the revenue coming in. It's crucial.

KEY STATS

Sixty-two percent of America's counties have public lands.

Just as crucial is our collaboration with the federal government. Take law enforcement, for instance. Our sheriff covers the county and the federal rangers police public campgrounds and things like that. Our sheriff has to coordinate with the rangers and persuade them that in Wyoming—like most states—the sheriff is recognized as the chief law enforcement person within the county. That said, it entails working very closely with federal law enforcement and coordinating their law enforcement capability with ours—whether it's the sheriff in pursuit of someone and having to cross onto public land or whether to avoid such things as a federal ranger citing somebody with a horse trailer out in the middle of nowhere with a broken taillight.

Again, collaboration is of primary importance because the economic base of our county is entangled with the federal government. Our three main sources of revenue are oil and natural gas, which mostly occur on federal land; agriculture, which encompasses federal land because of the grazing permits that ranchers use; and recreation.

In order to have a year-round operation, the cattle are usually on private land from October until approximately early May. Then they graze on federal land. Normally, they go to land below the forest. In early July, they move to our grazing allotment on land administered by the Forest Service. They remain there until mid-September, and then it's back to private land. They have to leave our land in the summer so we can put the hay up, which is what we use as a resource to keep the cattle through the winter.

In addition, the wildlife depend on private and public land. In the winter, they use our land to stay alive. That's where the rivers are and the willows, the shelter. We also divert water from the rivers for irrigation. The unused irrigation water provides return flow back to the river. This has changed our streams from being intermittent—in other words, they only run for a while when the snow melts—to perennial streams, which run all the time because of the return flow from agricultural use.

There are numerous recreational opportunities here. We adjoin Yellowstone Park, and a lot of the tourists come to our county to use our public lands. Hiking and off-road vehicles are very popular in the summer and snowmobiling in the winter. We have numerous outfitters that lead guided hunts, generally for people who come from back east. Almost all of that occurs on public land. Then we have hunters who come on their own and get permission to access private land to get through to the public land. We do that on our ranch, allow access for hunters to go through our property to the forest.

The county benefits because the visitors spend money in our motels and restaurants and they significantly help our economy. This is just a brief look at the customs and culture of our community. I learned how important both are being a rancher and by working a significant amount of time with the range staff of federal agencies. In fact, probably more than anything else, that's what prompted me to run for a seat on the county commission. At the time, I noticed that the commissioners on the board didn't realize how critical their participation could be in helping preserve our customs and culture.

I never thought a set solution to all our troubles existed. But the first step is for the counties to engage with the federal government. You have to get to know their people and develop a relationship with them. We meet with state and federal agencies once a month. We have a breakfast meeting and just talk about issues, our plans, the challenges to the budget; you name it, we talk about it. The only way you develop the level of trust required is by working closely with people, making decisions with them by looking at the same piece of ground together, and then fixing the problem as best you can. When you do that together, you develop an enhanced level of trust. So, when something does come up out of the blue, no one is afraid to pick up the phone. I never hesitate to call my Bureau of Land Management field manager to discuss anything that may be going on.

I always tell other commissioners, especially new commissioners or even anyone thinking about running for a board, you start by learning and understanding the customs and culture of your county. You have to ask yourself: "What does my county do?" You're going to need a budget to provide services, so where does the money come from? How do you nourish your economic base? Because if you don't do that, you won't have the budget to do things you're required to do.

All of this means you can't work in isolation. Look at everybody around you who is responsible for management decisions and then work with them in a collaborative way to solve problems. And do your networking. Go to NACo meetings. NACo has been extremely effective in supporting federal policy that helps provide counties the tools they need to have a seat at the table addressing issues with the federal agencies. I've got the numbers of everybody I might have to talk to in my cell phone. I call them and they call me. When I reflect on it, sometimes we get more done informally—eating lunch or sitting around the bar in the evening or just having conversations with commissioners or with representatives of the federal agencies from D.C.

I can reduce my advice to a little formula: collaboration and communication equals trust.

PARKS AND RECREATION

Parks and Recreation Director Amanda Heidecker
Leon County, Florida

"It is a lovely Leon County park with a wonderful story to tell as a project of reclamation and rebirth."

Beginning in 2006, I was a scholarship athlete on the women's cross-country team at Florida State University (FSU). Our home meets were held at Miccosukee Greenway, located just five miles from the state capitol in Tallahassee. It's a linear park with about six miles of a wide gravel path through pasture and woodlands alongside roads crossing urban and suburban communities. It is very popular with joggers, hikers, mountain bikers, and horseback riders. Between our FSU and high school cross-country meets, the races grew, with hundreds of runners and thousands of spectators. Traffic was disrupted for nearby homeowners, and crowds began to be a problem. People complained, loudly. It was apparent that we had outgrown Miccosukee Greenway, a Leon County park, and we needed to find a new home to host the meets—not a simple thing, since cross-country courses require miles of trails and hundreds of acres.

Word spread to Leon County government officials that Florida State was looking for a new locale. The university's track and field coaches connected with Gulf Winds Track Club. The club's leaders had a piece of property in mind and invited Florida State coaches to visit it. Imagine the expression on the coaches' faces when they saw the sign to the Leon County Solid Waste Facility—better known by locals as "the dump."

They soon learned that the facility was composed of more than 600 acres, and the portion they were envisioning as a cross-country site was about 120 acres of undeveloped land, including pastureland and pine forests. That portion had never been used as a landfill. In fact, Leon County officials were beginning discussions about eventually closing the solid waste facility. The timing was fortuitous for the cross-country teams desperate for a home, so what had seemed like a far- fetched idea soon became reality.

KEY STATS

Counties invest annually $12 billion to build and maintain parks and recreational facilities.

The undeveloped 120-acre portion was renamed Apalachee Regional Park, and the first cross-country meet at the venue was held in 2009. It was not the most ideal running locale because it was mostly a narrow, single-track trail. I made the best of the new cross-country venue, which was substandard compared to other Division I programs. I graduated from Florida State in 2010. In my senior year, I had an internship with the Leon County Division of Tourism (Visit Tallahassee). After three years in sports sales, I was hired by the division.

An upward trend for the Apalachee Regional Park cross-country venue began in 2010 when Florida State University and Gulf Winds Track Club each presented $10,000 to the Leon County Board of County Commissioners to make improvements. That $20,000 was used to widen the cross-country course. When that was complete, the course could accommodate hundreds of cross-country runners at the same time. My position with the Division of Tourism put me in the thick of the planning. Because I was a Florida State alumna and a cross-country runner who had competed at the highest collegiate level, my input was valued. Our overall goal was to create a first-rate course that could one day host the NCAA Division I National Cross-Country Championships.

The first challenge was to widen the entire course to ten meters, a requirement for hosting the NCAA Championship. It was more challenging and more expensive than it sounded because the back part of the course went through a forest and the trees were so tightly packed that it was barely wide enough to let a golf cart drive through. A lot of tree-and-stump removal and other excavation work was required. After many meetings and discussion, we cleared that hurdle thanks to a $250,000 investment from the Leon County Board of County Commissioners, which embraced our vision. That was when improvements began to accelerate. In 2013, we hosted the Florida High School Athletic Association State Championship at Apalachee Regional Park.

Our vision not only took the runner into consideration, but we also put a strong focus on the spectator experience. Watching a cross-country meet often involves spectators trudging through a forest after the start in order to catch a small portion of your runner's race and the finish, and we created excellent vantage points and cut-through paths. We also invested in technology throughout the course in order to take us to the national championship level. We installed a fiber optic line through the entire two-mile loop of the course, which allows us to plug in cameras to capture live action footage of the runners and to enhance the ability to clock accurate times at each portion of the course. We set up nine separate cameras that deliver a livestream of the race to the huge jumbotron screen, which can be viewed by thousands of spectators from more than 100 yards away.

These upgrades have been a game-changer. For the past six years, every one of the major cross-country races that we hosted has been live streamed so it can be watched online, and many are also broadcast on cable television. That has given us the opportunity to market and promote our course and to elevate the recognition of Apalachee Regional Park and Leon County.

The steady, upward trajectory of the facility has exceeded our most optimistic expectations. We have drawn crowds of more than 10,000 spectators to some of our races, which is a boom for tourism, bringing revenue to hotel operators, restaurant owners, and other local merchants while allowing the county to use hotel-bed occupancy taxes to reinvest in the community. Those tourism tax revenue funds have been used to pay for further improvements to the cross-country course and the infrastructure.

For example, after the solid waste facility was shut down, a portion of the former landfill was capped and turned into parking lots that can accommodate up to 4,000 vehicles. The course topography is challenging, with hills and elevation changes of up to fifty feet, but it is not overly grueling, and the runners give the course high praise. We also varied the trails with different surfaces, including manicured grass similar to golf-course turf on the front portion and a unique surface on the back portion. Oysters are prevalent in Apalachicola, located about an hour south of Leon County. We utilized crushed oyster shells on the back portion of the course. They pack together with a tight bond and also drain well after heavy rains. Crushed oyster shells make for a strong cross-country surface you won't find anywhere else.

The tourism tax revenue continues to fund improvements, including a new restroom and operations facility, an award stage, a finish line structure, and fencing that defines the course. In 2021, the Leon County Division of Tourism fulfilled our dream of hosting the NCAA Division I National Cross-Country Championships, the first time the championships had been held in Florida in the program's 83-year history. Building on this success, Leon County was selected to host the 2026 World Cross-Country Championships at Apalachee Regional Park. My colleagues in Leon County's Division of Tourism and Parks and Recreation department have forged important relationships and collaborations with our local business owners, who understand the economic engine that we provide. We show appreciation, respect, and passion for a sport I have been deeply involved with for much of my life. This, in turn, has fostered goodwill, cemented the community's support, and ensured a durable relationship.

Equally important, Apalachee Regional Park is considered a gem for multiple uses and has become a haven for walkers, hikers, dog walkers, and bikers. Soon, the landfill will be closed entirely and all 600 acres will be restored to parkland. We are in the process of building additional biking and hiking trails and we'll be creating a dog park.

One of the favorite parts of my job is that I regularly run the course. I love to hear the crunch of the ground-up oyster shells and the soft footfalls on turf when I move onto the grass portion of the loop. The scenery is varied and beautiful, including wide open pastureland and canopy oak trees whose leaves block direct sunlight and cloak portions of the trail with cool shade as it wends through forestland. It is a lovely Leon County park with a wonderful story to tell as a project of reclamation and rebirth.

It is such a lovely landscape that I often forget it used to be a landfill.

COMMUNITY
AND
ECONOMICS

ECONOMIC DEVELOPMENT

Regional Economic Growth Director Stuart Clason
Utah Association of Counties

"Economic development requires a team approach."

Economic development people are quick to tell you how many jobs they've created and how much capital investment they've attracted. However, economic development people don't do that—companies do. Economic development people should not be giving away everything in exchange for jobs and investment. Instead, they should make sure that they're receiving the jobs and investment that align with the values and history of the communities they are assisting.

When I played baseball in high school, I'd always take a pinch of the infield dirt and eat it. It's weird, I know. But I did it because the dirt is different on every field and I wanted to know its taste. That's similar to the first step of economic development. You must take the time to learn about your communities, the people, and their problems. All twenty-nine counties of our state are members of our association. For the past three years, we have been building relationships and a platform that took into account the differences among the counties.

Our approach is to make it clear to the communities we work with that we have to work on a regional level and support each other. The fact is I can't do anything to help if the communities don't buy in. Economic development requires a team approach. My first year I logged 50,000 miles of driving because that's the other thing you have to do—show up. People want to see your eyes and size you up.

Utah has a highly urbanized area, which is primarily Salt Lake County, but also includes the shoulder counties that make up what's known as the Wasatch Front. But 30 percent of the state's population lives in Salt Lake County and that's where 50 percent of the jobs are located. The smaller counties just don't have the capacity to plan growth and development on their own. They tell us what they want, and we provide the technical assistance and the strategy to pursue their vision.

KEY STATS

The top industries in 2019 in Carbon County, Utah, were mining, quarrying and oil, gas extraction; real estate, and government enterprises.

One of our first projects was in a coal-reliant community, Carbon County. In its heyday, I believe the county had eighty active coal mines; today, there are none. They did have railway infrastructure that had been used for shipping coal and a company, Intermountain Electronics (IE), founded by a gentleman named John Houston. His number one client had been the mines. When we started meeting with him and his CEO, IE was a $100 million a year company with an eight-year plan mapped out to take them to $500 million a year. IE builds sophisticated electrical systems for data centers. The company was expanding their corporate office and manufacturing capacity and they were considering Denver because oil and gas was also a big customer.

Mr. Houston approached the county and said his company had an incentive package to expand in Denver, which had a good labor force to pull from, but he would love to talk to us about what we could put together for the company to expand in Utah. I drank a lot of coffee with Mr. Houston. He and I became friends. He was born and raised in that community. He's multigenerational. And what we talked about is the difference between that community and Denver.

A downside to expanding to Denver was that it's hard to build a company culture in a big labor market because your employees will jump for twenty-five cents more an hour. The CEO of IE lived in Denver and was adamant about expanding there. We had to get within the range of the Denver offer. We put together a package that included a reduction in property tax. Then we worked with the state, which agreed to the largest, rural post-performance income-and-tax incentive they had ever awarded. My partner and I built the financial models.

I told John Houston that the incentives were the easy part. Far tougher would be creating a pipeline to furnish the hundreds of new employees his company would need. We turned to Utah State University, which has a regional campus in the county, and created a curriculum funded and supported by Utah State and delivered at IE. The classroom is the floor of IE's manufacturing facility. Now, students can receive a subsidized education. Juniors in high school can begin working at IE and in three years they can earn a high school diploma and an associate's degree. Then, if they choose to work for IE, they can. If they don't, they can work somewhere else.

The next problem was the housing shortage. We started working with Price, the largest city in Carbon County. Luckily, a local businessman who owned a lot of acreage wanted to build a housing development for a while, so John Houston offered to furnish the down payment for young people to build a house in exchange for them signing a five-year employment agreement with IE.

I was proud of what was accomplished. I'm from a rural community that's dead and never coming back to life because the business leaders and elected officials were scared to let in outsiders. The last time we were home, we went to the church next to my parents' house for Thanksgiving dinner. Our children were with us, and they were the only children in the church. It was sad for me because all around us I saw the people who had helped raise me.

Rural communities, even when they try to attract business, struggle. For example, there has been a proliferation of solar projects in Utah. Solar developers wanted property-tax incentives. They were focusing on communities that didn't know how to negotiate with them and the developers were shaping the incentives. Early on, solar developers were getting 70 percent of the new tax revenue as a direct incentive. We stepped in to partner with county elected officials and fought tooth and nail to greatly reduce that number to 20-45 percent, which increases the tax revenue going to local taxing entities like school districts.

Rural communities need someone who understands their situation. Because they don't have an abundance of population, they are always working—running sprinkler lines, moving cattle, volunteering to coach Little League. They don't have a lot of spare time. If you call a meeting, it better include some action items. You can't talk down to them and act as if you know all the answers. And when you say you are going to do something, you better do it.

The biggest issue Utah is dealing with—one that I suspect agricultural communities around the country are confronting—is the generational changeover. Traditionally, in Utah, due to the Church of Jesus Christ of Latter-day Saints, you have large families. So how do you carve up the acreage in a responsible way? And then, there is the generational handover where the younger generation wants to come in and innovate, but the present generation has a hard time letting go.

Whatever these rural communities are facing, it is fulfilling to work with them. The social fabric is tighter than in urban areas because it has to be—they have fewer resources. Once the people trust you, they'll invite you into their homes, and it's an honor to build these relationships with some of the most authentic people I've ever met in my life. I don't see them as business partners. I see them as part of my family. If I let them down, I'm letting down my aunt or uncle or cousins.

I think the next wave of what we will be doing is creating more public-private partnerships—PPPs, as they are called. The question for us to answer is how do we take our state and national foundations and government resources and align them with state money? Utah has more than twenty banks, and the Community Reinvestment Act requires them to put one percent of their total deposits in community-related investments. We have to figure out the best way to combine those three pools and create capital stacks that can go toward addressing housing needs across the state and, specifically, in rural areas. Or we could go back and work with a company like Intermountain Electronics and build a cluster of companies in the region that could supply Intermountain Electronics. That's where we will focus.

Tourism will be a major part of this work moving forward. We're only four to five hours from six national parks and an entry point for people who want to explore the West. I personally don't know how it will all align. The COVID-19 pandemic showed us that if you're an economy solely based on tourism, you're in a bind, but you also need to be realistic about what your existing economic drivers are and how to leverage them. We have been interfacing with the tourism community because they are an important factor when it comes to real-estate development and it's good for the two sides to be hand in glove. That's going to be the next wave of success in our program. That, and remembering that diversifying rural communities is the best way to secure their futures.

EMPLOYMENT

**Oakland County Michigan Works! Director and
Workforce Development Manager Jennifer Llewellyn**
Oakland County, Michigan

*"All of us are one terrible moment away from facing the same
predicament as the people who come to us for help."*

On a June morning in 1997, my father went to work and the door was padlocked. The company went under without notifying the employees. Dad had worked there as a burr machinist for close to twenty years. He was a Vietnam veteran without a high school diploma. In October, my mother was laid off from her job as an executive secretary to a plant manager. I was a sophomore at Oakland University. My brother was in high school.

My parents started using the Michigan Works! office in Troy. Mom received training and added computer skills to her resume, and they helped my dad find work. I was working a boring part-time job. Mom suggested I talk to a career advisor at the Troy office. I went to see him, and he said they were looking for summer interns to coach students. I accepted an internship and soon found my passion.

Later on, I became a career advisor, then a program coordinator, a director of the Troy center, and now I oversee all of the Michigan Works! offices. But if there has been one constant that informs our efforts and partially explains our success, it is the knowledge that all of us are one terrible moment away from facing the same predicament as the people who come to us for help.

Oakland County is part of the metropolitan Detroit area. We have approximately 44,000 businesses and 1.3 million residents. The county produces 20 percent of Michigan's gross domestic product. The automakers are here and so are most of their Tier 1 suppliers, so the economic ups and downs of the automotive industry are felt keenly. I can recall the first Chrysler outplacement in 2001. About 1,500 workers were laid off, primarily engineers and other white-collar employees. The culture was still that you stayed with one company for your career. I'll never forget working with those individuals; many of them were completely paralyzed by the thought of a job search and hadn't prepared a resume in thirty years. I assisted with reformatting resumes and we printed them out on nice paper. I helped some people start school or guided them toward government training programs.

KEY STATS

Counties are involved in 90 percent of the country's 550 local workforce development boards. Around 28 percent of workforce development boards are within a county department or function as a county department.

Today, more people than ever are quitting their jobs and looking to improve their lives by using technologies that free them to work from home or, in some cases, to work in any place they want regardless of where the company is located. Businesses are also considering new models, asking themselves, "Do I need this building? Do I need people to live where we work?" For a number of businesses, the answer to these questions is a resounding no, and all of this creates opportunities.

The Michigan Works! Association has sixteen regional locations. I oversee the Oakland County branch. We provide development services to businesses and job seekers, and right now have about forty-seven different grants totaling about $30 million. We have programs for youth, businesses, and individuals who have been laid off and who are receiving cash or food assistance benefits. Our goal is to deliver these services in a one-stop shop through our six Michigan Works! offices, so they're spread strategically around the county, particularly in communities with underrepresented populations inaccessible through public transportation. Any business or job seeker can call, visit, or email our offices and feel comfortable admitting they are unsure what to do next and they will receive help with their job search. It could be tuition to return to school and complete a degree or earn a certification or one-on-one job search assistance. For employers, sometimes it's layoff support or hiring support or retention issues. We are matchmakers between employers and potential employees.

Our workforce development board is extraordinary. These individuals commit their personal time to making certain we're moving in the right direction as far as the services we offer. We have a fantastic county executive, David Coulter, who has made workforce a top priority. The executive and the board and the business and nonprofit leaders are really the visionaries behind our successful workforce system, and it's because of them that we have a reputation statewide and nationally as being so innovative.

It is a good time to be in workforce development. We are seeing a big demand from General Motors, Ford, Chrysler, Nissan, Toyota, and their suppliers as they transition from traditional combustion engineers to software and electrical engineering. In fact, businesses are desperately seeking talent. In Michigan, we have lost almost 200,000 women in the workforce during the two plus years of the pandemic and our employers, especially in female-dominated occupations—retail, hospitality, and nursing—have been extraordinarily impacted.

The primary sectors we focus on are the health-sciences industry, information technology, advanced manufacturing, and construction, which includes transportation and logistics. Oakland County Community College has been a longtime strategic partner in the two-year associate degree space and in some industry-recognized credentials and certificates. My alma mater, Oakland University, has also been a terrific partner, leading the way in the health sciences and engineering programs. We have great labor organizations across the county and numerous nonprofit partners.

Two years ago, we set a goal we call Oakland80. Our goal, by 2030, is for 80 percent of our county's adult residents to have an industry-recognized certificate, credential, or degree. At the moment, we are at

61 percent, the second-highest in the state behind Washtenaw County, which is home to the University of Michigan. Admittedly, it is an ambitious goal, but we are working closely with our K-12 partners, colleges, universities, proprietary schools, and labor unions. We have apprenticeship programs and not just the traditional ones like plumbing, but new apprenticeships for software developers, truck drivers—a top in-demand job in our area—and medical assistants thanks to Henry Ford Health System, a major health system in Southeast Michigan. To make sure people are aware of their options, we publish an apprenticeship guide.

We brought 10,000 high school students to a large venue so they could see and touch different career occupations. The bricklayers union came and the kids could build brick walls. The operating engineers came with their simulators and the kids had a chance to operate a backhoe simulator. The plumbers union came and showed them how to unplug a toilet. This is how we spread awareness to youth and adults about options for credentials and sustainable careers that will lead to economic self-sufficiency.

Some time ago, Amazon tore down the Pontiac Silverdome, where the Detroit Lions used to play, and built a massive facility. A substantial number of robots in the United States are built and designed there. We partnered with the community college to create a fifteen-week robotics-and-automation certification program. Tuition costs $8,000 a person, but we cover that through grants. Then, two of our major health systems, Beaumont Health and Henry Ford Health, told us they couldn't find sterile processing technicians (SPTs), so we went to the college and they created an SPT program. We're placing students in that program; they're providing the training, and then the health systems are hiring the students upon completion. We're now working on a new cybersecurity certificate and a new certified nursing-assistant certificate using the same approach. The training programs are employer-driven. That enables the students to find a job when they graduate. We take the same approach with our apprenticeships. We're working on a child-development associate apprenticeship program. We know the childcare industry was hit hard during the pandemic. Michigan alone needs 10,000 new licensed childcare providers to fill the need for affordable childcare. We're close to getting a child development associate apprenticeship program off the ground. I'm particularly proud that we don't just talk about challenges and publish reports, but we create solutions for our residents and our companies by having business, education, and government working together.

Soon we'll be launching Oakland80 career navigators. We expect to deploy between six and twelve career navigators across the county. Any resident can meet with this career and educational navigator and glean some insight and guidance on careers and education options. We think this will be attractive to parents for themselves and maybe for their older children. We know there is this pocket of eighteen to twenty-four-year-olds who are disengaged from school and the workforce and we want to reach that group. Parents are critical in targeting that population.

Last year, we started a program that expunges some criminal records for residents. Of course, not everyone is eligible. We have an attorney on our staff who provides the expungement services at no cost, and the letters he has received have brought us to tears—people thanking him for an opportunity they never thought possible. In fact, we receive these types of letters from many men and women we have helped—letters telling us that we have changed their lives for the better, and personally, these compliments make all of my efforts worthwhile.

AFFORDABLE HOUSING

Commissioner David Montgomery
Williams County, North Dakota

"We no longer hesitate to ask developers hard questions about their plans."

I was born in 1956 and I've lived here my whole life. Today, the county has a population of approximately 44,000, three-quarters of whom live in the city of Williston, our county seat. During my lifetime, we have gone through three oil booms and busts. I was too young to remember the first one, but I do recall the second cycle during the late 1970s. It didn't last long, maybe two or three years. As the 1980s boom began, we needed housing. The city of Williston issued special tax assessments to pay for infrastructure to support new developments, but after the boom went bust, the city got stuck holding the bag to the tune of some $100 million.

It took twenty years for everybody who was left here to pay the debt off and somewhere around 2010, before the final payment on the earlier debt, there was another boom. Thank God this time around the city didn't attempt to do any special improvements with taxpayer money, and all the developers were pretty much on their own as far as paying for infrastructure.

Williams County is primarily—like North Dakota itself—agricultural. Our main crops are durum and spring wheat. After the boom and bust in the 1980s, we still had a little drilling going on, but the Williston area returned to being good old small town, rural USA, a friendly community where you knew your neighbors. Our biggest headache was that when kids graduated high school they went off and never returned, understandable because we had a limited job market. So then we had a number of houses that were empty and two trailer parks that were completely closed.

───── **KEY STATS** ─┐

Counties invest $12.8 billion annually in housing and community development.

My wife and I have two daughters. By 2005, they were off at college and my wife and I believed they would never move back to Williston. Then, the next boom hit around 2009. Our daughters returned and they are still here. Their husbands work in the oil industry. Williston alone went from 11,000 people to over 30,000 people in less than a year and housing was one of the main challenges for people coming here to work. Because we remembered what happened in previous boom and busts, city and county leaders were leery of taking on any long-term debt to support housing development. What was sad and frustrating for me was that we had a lot of elderly living in apartment complexes and their rent soared from let's say $200 to $1,000 a month. Retired people on fixed incomes struggle to pay that high of an increase.

That meant private investors showed up and suddenly the county commission meetings were dragging on for six or seven hours, and probably 90 percent of those meetings dealt with planning and zoning. Everybody was coming here to make a buck. By natural inclination, those of us who grew up in the county trusted people and we often did business on a handshake, but what we learned in the 2010s was that there were people appearing before us who weren't so trustworthy.

Developers would buy agricultural land. At that time, ag land in the county was maybe $500 an acre. Now, they start offering to pay anywhere from $5,000 to $30,000 an acre! Next, the developer would show up at the county commission meeting to get their land rezoned for developments—residential or industrial or commercial. We didn't have strict guidelines until 2012, so in the early years they got their rezoning and before you knew it, they had flipped the land for a profit and we ended up with industrial projects sitting beside new homes. It was a mess.

Some farmers refused to sell and they wound up living next door to industrial buildings. They were so angry at their neighbors for selling that it ruined longtime friendships. But if you're a farmer with that kind of money in front of you, sometimes it's hard to turn it down.

All of this made the pursuit of affordable housing frustrating and when developers came before the commission to do their song and dance claiming they would offer affordable housing in their development, I asked them if they could define that term. None of them bothered until finally one of them said, "Affordable housing is what the market dictates." That, in my opinion, wasn't quite true because it excluded people who weren't working in oil and gas.

For all intents and purposes, when the booms started, we had no building department and only a part-time planning-and-zoning individual. By 2011, we realized that we had to staff up and now, between those two departments, we have nine employees. In July of 2012, we added a code-enforcement officer. That was necessary because by then we had makeshift man camps happening in parks and on abandoned farmsteads and RVs were infuriating residents by parking outside their houses. It was the employers' responsibility to secure safe and reasonable places for their employees to live. Two deserted trailer parks from an earlier boom were purchased, revitalized and quickly filled with hundreds of mobile homes.

Not all of the projects were an unqualified success. I mentioned that RVs were being parked everywhere. Well, this guy had an idea to build a facility on a hill six or seven miles north of Williston, basically a campground with room for some three hundred RVs. Hindsight, as we know, is 20/20, but I would never approve something like this again. We had people living out there in the middle of winter and some of them froze to death or got asphyxiated because they brought a kerosene or propane heater into their RVs. On top of that, when I drove up to the top of the hill in summertime, it became apparent to me that if one of our usual prairie fires broke out and we got northwest winds, the fire would sweep through the campground in ten minutes. It scared me to death.

Another ill-advised project was the Epping Ranch. A developer planned to build one hundred houses, and by 2014 or 2015, after twenty or thirty were completed, oil and gas went through a downturn and development was abandoned. The homes were mortgaged to the hilt. The owners couldn't make the payments, so the houses went back to the banks and they are mostly sitting empty today.

The overwhelming majority of workers flooding into the county in 2011 and 2012 were single males. Without available housing, many of them were living in their cars; they wanted to have fun when they were done working, so the bars were packed. Crime and drug use jumped. Most of the workers were decent guys, but a small percentage of them weren't and our sheriff needed more deputies. Eventually, we had to expand our jail from six cells with thirty beds, which generally handled weekend drunks, to a facility with 240 beds. Within three years, we doubled the number of deputies. In order to recruit, we needed a stable place for deputies to live, away from the folks they dealt with every night, so the county purchased three-bedroom mobile homes in one of the reopened trailer parks and rented rooms to newly hired staff.

In addition to deputies, we needed more accounting and administrative workers. Yet we couldn't afford to pay the same wages that employers were paying their oil workers and our new public employees would have to compete for housing with them, a difficult proposition. By the summer of 2012, it was obvious to the commissioners that the housing shortage constrained our ability to respond to the boom. We decided that, although our next big project was slated to be a county highway complex, it was wiser to shelve that plan and put up a building with offices on the main floor with apartments above. At the same time, the city of Williston partnered with the developer in the construction of an apartment complex and got priority in renting those units. Every employer was scrambling to find a housing solution for their staff. Unfortunately, although we weren't receiving a reasonable portion of the oil and gas production tax, we had to solve the issues of the oil boom locally. Starting in 2013, we worked with the legislature to adjust the formula for distributing oil-and-gas production taxes to ensure that the taxes collected by the state of North Dakota are allocated back to the region impacted by oil production.

Fortunately, this boom has lasted longer than the others. Families are deciding to settle here and riding out the tough times, if they come. So now we have to manage sustained long-term growth that requires housing and the amenities that go with raising a family. Our school enrollment had a drastic increase—honestly, the system was overwhelmed at one point. We figured the enrollment would drop when our economy slowed down due to the pandemic, but surprisingly there was no decrease.

The good news is that the latest round of industrial development will establish Williams County as home to a petrochemical industrial corridor, so there will be more jobs— stable jobs. We have billions of dollars of development underway in the southwest corner of the county, a pocket that is somewhat untouched by oil and housing development. We are prepared to help this area with the challenges of new development. We have the planning and zoning procedures to manage development and we are more proactive. We no longer hesitate to ask developers hard questions about their plans. Just as important, we have thicker skins and, sadly, no longer automatically assume that people seeking to do business in the county should be trusted.

ELECTIONS

Clerk/Auditor Ricky Hatch
Weber County, Utah

"We care about doing a good job because we believe elections are one of the pillars, along with the law, of our civil society."

I have a confession: Election officials are control freaks. We have backup plans for our backup plans, checklists to track all of our checklists, and statistics all over the place, all of which are necessary to protect the system from unforeseen circumstances and bad actors. It's also helpful to like dealing with numbers. I do. Before I was elected in 2010, I worked as a certified public accountant. Still, nothing in my background prepared me for the COVID pandemic or the decrease in voter confidence, which is especially acute right now, and one of the biggest problems I face.

Overall, in Utah, 81 percent of voters are confident that our elections are run properly, but we still have a problem in our state, which is predominantly Republican. There is a small, super-vocal group who still believe there was fraud in 2020. They stir the pot and many other voters get a little worried. The Massachusetts Institute of Technology analyzed voter confidence and found that there is a 20 to 30 percent swing in whether voters trust the outcome of an election, which depends entirely upon on whether their candidate won or lost. We saw that big time in the last election.

It's difficult to counter this skepticism and to find a way to educate the public about the controls we have in place. Our neighboring county conducts an Election Integrity Night, a tour every month. We began publicizing and conducting monthly tours. I sent an open invitation on Facebook to over 20,000 people. The newspaper published the invite. We put the events all over social media. Still, fewer than 10 people come and almost all of them are election deniers, already convinced that our processes and equipment are compromised.

KEY STATS

Every two years, counties fund and oversee more than 100,000 polling places and coordinate nearly 800,000 poll workers.

Managing an election is daunting. Weber County has 115,000 voters. Before Utah became a primarily-vote-by-mail state, our county had to recruit over 600 poll workers, vet them, hire them, train them, deploy them, and pay them. We would bring them in for two to four hours of training. We tried to verify that they understand the key points of their position. It's hard to expose them to all of the things they might see at the polls without overwhelming them. On Election Day, we deployed them, and hoped that they would function perfectly. If they make a mistake, they could disenfranchise a voter and disenfranchisement is the dirtiest word in an election official's vocabulary. We'll do anything we can to avoid it.

You'd think with the partisan complaining about elections, political parties would be eager to provide poll workers. Not so. They also have a hard time finding someone willing to work a fifteen-hour day for twelve bucks an hour. People who sign up to be a poll worker don't do it for the money; they love our country and they want to serve.

One best practice, if your state allows it, is to recruit high school students. In Utah, sixteen and seventeen-year-olds are permitted to be poll workers even though they can't vote. We also recruit students from Weber State University, which is in Weber County. The students have been fantastic. We use them as rovers and troubleshooters when poll workers have problems with their laptops or iPads. Unlike us older folks, the students are comfortable with technology and they roam among our different polling places, solving problems.

In some parts of the country, counties have reached out to local businesses and asked them to "sponsor" a polling place and donate their employees' time to run it. I've heard that this practice works quite well. Many states have passed laws that forbid the use of private money in elections, which may put an end to this practice. Counties with heavy in-person voting demands almost always struggle to hire enough poll workers.

Because our county and state conduct our elections primarily by mail, our need for poll workers has been significantly reduced and we have a nice, trusted group of workers with years of experience. Although we're always glad when new people apply, we are more likely to use workers with experience. Almost all of our training is now online. We send out links to videos that explain the key processes and show each step, focusing quite a bit on setting up the electronic poll books and checking in voters. You have to do it exactly right or the equipment won't function properly and the voter won't get the correct ballot.

No matter how careful we are, voters can get testy. In 2020, one woman called me a liar because I'd stated that everyone has the option to vote in person, and she said, "I went in person and I was turned away." I asked her why, and she replied, "Because I wouldn't wear a mask."

I explained that mask-wearing had nothing to do with elections; it was a health order from our county health department, and I couldn't control that. I also mentioned that our poll workers were instructed to allow everyone to vote, even if they didn't have a mask. I suspect she either didn't actually come to vote in person or she misunderstood our poll workers' instructions. I don't get into screaming matches. I smile and try to find something that I can agree with them on. "Yes," I'll say, "elections are crucial, and I do everything in my power to make sure they are run objectively, securely, and accurately." However, that doesn't satisfy everyone.

I remember the Sunday before Election Day in 2020. I was in church and stood up and said, "All hands on deck. If anyone can come down to the county office, we need help tearing the tabs off sealed envelopes." This task is perfunctory, extremely repetitive and, frankly, quite boring.

We had adults and kids, maybe thirty people, helping us remove the tabs. It took us nearly four hours to remove the tabs from the approximately 20,000 envelopes. The next morning, our staff completed the next step in the process, which was to compare the signatures on the envelopes to those we had on file. We provide special training for people to do that. We're fortunate here because the county purchased an envelope processor. This purchase strained our budget, but was well worth the cost. The equipment takes an image of the voter's signature on the envelope and automatically verifies signatures that are obvious matches. Signatures that are not clear matches are compared manually by a team of election workers trained in signature comparison.

Looking ahead, voter confidence and public trust will be our highest hurdles. Over the past 25 years, our country went from paper punch-card ballots to touchscreen voting machines, and now back to paper ballots. Having a paper record is crucial to safeguard and audit the accuracy of the process. Many older people love going to the polls in person. They love the comradery, the patriotism they feel when they do it, and seeing their ballots scanned into a machine or dropped into a ballot box.

Online voting is a very different situation. It will probably take years for the technology to get to where it can be verifiably secure, and even longer before voters are willing to trust it. I think the younger generation will demand it—they already are. Some jurisdictions, such as Jackson County, Oregon and Utah County in Utah, already use it for military and overseas voters. This technology provides an option to a small number of voters who can't vote in person and who can't return a paper ballot. We will continue to see it slowly expand. Although I like the concept of online voting, it still has a long road before it becomes widely used.

Those of us in charge of overseeing elections are becoming more collaborative with each other. We communicate more often and share best practices. In the past, you had to attend a conference to learn about the latest developments. Today, it's all up on the web, and we are quicker to implement shared ideas. Election administration is starting to mature as an industry, but staying current is still difficult for small jurisdictions. Seventy percent of jurisdictions have fewer than 30,000 voters. Their election departments are limited—one person, maybe two. In many cases, it's a part-time official, and there is no IT person to provide technical support. Today, though, we can more easily reach them, and best practices, technology, and innovative ideas are far more accessible to election officials across the country, regardless of their jurisdiction's size.

As for those who doubt the integrity of our elections, I wish they could see the level of care and effort that we put into making sure that voting is secure, accurate, and trustworthy. Election officials care much more about the process than about who wins. We all feel this way, regardless of what party we belong to or what our political leanings are. At conferences, election officials get together for dinner, totally geek out over election conversation for hours, and then marvel at the fact that during the whole discussion, nobody ever mentioned politics. In fact, I rarely know the party that most of my election colleagues belong to. That's because we focus exclusively on the process, not the outcome. I wish those who doubt could be at the table with us. They would quickly recognize that election officials have no agenda and no desire to promote one party or one candidate over another.

The last thing election officials want is to have an influence on the outcome of an election—we just want to get it done right. We're just normal people. We're your neighbors. We coach your children in Little League, go to church with you, and shop at the same grocery store. We care about doing a good job because we believe elections are one of the pillars, along with the law, of our civil society. We certainly don't do this work for the money or because it's a cushy job. For us, it's a passion and an expression of our belief in, and our hope for, our amazing country.

TRANSPORTATION

COUNTY ROADS

Board Member Denise Winfrey

Will County, Illinois

"Being a transportation hub is both a blessing and a curse."

Traffic. Our residents constantly complain about not only the level, but also the type of traffic. And I certainly understand. I've lived in Joliet, our county seat, since grade school when my family moved here from Southern Illinois. I attended college in Joliet, did my graduate work in Washington, D.C., and Cleveland, and then worked in private industry. By the time I helped my company through its sale and received a buyout, I was fifty. My father had been a teacher, my mother had been involved with the community and I wanted to enter public service. I started out with organizations like Rotary, and later on I was asked to fill a seat on a township board. Then, in 2009, my representative on the county board died and a friend encouraged me to run for the seat and I was elected.

My past, when our local roads were less jammed, is never far away from my memory. Our county building used to house Sears. When I was in high school, I worked there as a sales clerk. Of course, back then, I didn't oversee transportation and no one complained to me about the traffic.

We are a collar county of Cook County, part of the Greater Chicago Metro Area, and our population is approximately 700,000—a 350 percent increase from when my family arrived. I can recall when the campus of the junior college was farmland and there were plenty of truck farms. Gradually, an expansion to the east, west, and south began. Then, people residing closer to Chicago discovered that it was less expensive to live out this way; you could get more house and land for your money and still keep your job downtown because we had commuter trains going into the city. We grew and grew and our current size alone accounts for some of the congestion, but the major shift has been to Will County as the largest inland port in North America. Being a transportation hub is both a blessing and a curse.

KEY STATS

Counties are involved in 78 percent of public transportation systems.

Being located in the middle of the country, it's easy for companies to ship goods in every direction. As a matter of fact, on Interstate 80, one of our busiest roads, 63 percent of the traffic passes through without stopping. That's a big part of what happens around here. A lot of our jobs are tied to warehousing and trucking. Amazon has a significant presence in the area; as does IKEA, Walmart and several logistics firms. We also have the Des Plaines River, which connects to the Mississippi. Heavy equipment is shipped on waterways. We also have high-speed rail for freight. On top of these shipping lanes, not too far away from us in Cook County, are two airports, Midway and O'Hare.

Whatever is being shipped—whether it's a small box of pens or a giant television screen—its trip begins with being loaded onto a truck, which is why I'm always hearing a loud chorus of "No more trucks!"

However, while residents are singing that song, they add a refrain familiar to anyone who has served on a county board: "Cut our taxes!"

I'd love to do both, but the revenue funding the county, the revenue that lets us pay for essentials like parks and senior programs without raising our tax rate, is directly tied to the jobs and industries that need the trucks our residents wish would disappear.

Yet the traffic problem was created by more than growth. It was that we allowed the trucking industries and logistics plants to set up shop before we improved our infrastructure. Our roadways were not strong enough or wide enough to accommodate all the additional traffic. Interstate 80 is now being widened from four to six lanes, about 10 years late. But our local county roads have not been widened or shored up to support all of that increased traffic. Some have the weight limits to support the trucks, but they lack the width.

Across the United States, counties are the biggest holders of roadways. But our area has a special challenge: so many of our county roads connect to state roads and interstates and that commercial traffic exits onto our roads. We have to be certain that we can handle the size of the trucks so they don't destroy our roads after we've fixed them, a shameful waste of tax dollars. Almost all our roads need to be widened with the addition of turn lanes, so our residents can navigate with cars and our school buses can safely complete their routes, and the trucks, once they have left the highways, don't have to cut through residential areas.

Just in the time that I've been on the board—for the last thirteen years—the transportation issues have tripled simply because of the type of companies moving into Will County and what seems like their infinite need to move goods. One of the most interesting things I learned was what the county actually controls and what belongs to the Illinois Department of Transportation (IDOT), and how we can partner with the IDOT on grants. We have no control over state and city roads, but I also learned that we can bring some visual pressure on those entities if we keep up with the weeds and the trash underneath the overpasses and fix the potholes. If the county does our job, then state and city officials get the message. This helps us because all the roads are so close together that if our residents spot an eyesore or get a flat from bouncing into a hole—even if it's not our responsibility—they will think we're collecting their taxes and not spending the money wisely. Many roads are multi-jurisdictional so residents and often officials are not clear on who owns what. What residents are sure of is that something needs to be done and they don't care who does it, just as long as it happens.

One of the most frustrating hurdles I've faced is securing funding for a road project. It takes so long to put the proposal together and even longer for the approval process that when you finally receive the funds you sometimes have to go back and re-engineer the first phase because with the passing of time, the original engineering study is no longer valid. So back you go to the drawing board and basically you're starting over—except the price has skyrocketed. A project that was going to cost you $3 million is now going to cost you $10 million because materials and labor costs have increased.

These are challenges associated with the busiest, most populated sections of our county and the residents who drive the roads. We have a municipal bus system and also Dial-a-Ride so that we can pick up people—mainly the elderly who are no longer driving or persons with disabilities—in order to transport them to their medical appointments in either Joliet or Chicago. Uber and Lyft are often unaffordable for these people and their availability is not as widespread as in some other areas. In the future, we want to expand as many local bus routes as we can to accommodate the most vulnerable—the disabled, the poor, and the elderly not only in the city, but in our rural communities; many of them are retired from farming or have leased out the land, but still live in their houses and are unable to get around.

This is a primary concern for me and a concern I want our county to address in the coming years. In our poorer areas, the need for transportation is especially acute. There are not convenient bus pickups and schedules. The buses arrive too far apart so if people miss their bus, they have to sit for an hour in an open-sided bus shelter. This is the Midwest. It gets cold here. That's not great for anyone, but particularly not for older residents. The population in these areas desperately needs reliable transportation because the grocery stores and drugstores are not near them. Nor are the hospitals and doctors' offices. How are they supposed get back and forth safely? The only answer is that we will have to provide the way.

My plan has been—and will continue to be—that our county makes sure we collect our fair share of state tax dollars. Services are expensive. Our task as a county board is to help our residents, regardless of what kind of help is needed. Roads, buses, you name it. I've never kidded myself that as a board we had, or will have, any other task before us. We find the money. We do what needs to be done. That's our job and it is what I have always tried to do.

ROADS AND BRIDGES

Judge Glen Whitley
Tarrant County, Texas

"If we are going to keep people moving here, then we have to keep them moving after they get here."

Except for three years in California, I've spent my life in North Texas. I'm an accountant by training and founded a CPA firm before I was elected a county commissioner in 1997. A decade later I became the county judge, meaning I preside over the commissioner's court.

Our county seat is the city of Fort Worth, and we are now the fifteenth largest county in the United States. Our population is over two million and it has almost doubled in the last thirty years, so naturally building and maintaining roads and bridges has jumped to the top of our to-do list.

The issues surrounding growth were evident in 1997 when I was first elected and I asked to be appointed to the Metropolitan Planning Organization (MPO). The MPO covers a dozen counties. Our mission was to look at projects, specifically to approve projects on the federal level as well as working closely with the state department of transportation and the local toll authority. We also worked with various cities and the county to help them maintain their arterials, and we have done bond projects leveraging county funds with city or state funds for new construction. During the twenty-five years I've been on the commissioner's court, we have gone through several federal programs, including receiving the largest Transportation Investment Generating Economic Recovery grants ever awarded.

In addition, we started P3 projects—public-private

partnerships—where the private sector built managed lanes, maintaining three lanes on either side of them and collecting tolls. We were one of the first counties in the state to take that approach. Furthermore, we managed to incentivize our cities and the state by putting up our bond money so they would put up their own dollars. That began in 2006, and I estimate that since then we have leveraged our $200 million to somewhere in the neighborhood of $600 to $800 million.

KEY STATS

Seventy-six percent of public roads across the nation are owned and maintained by local governments.

It wasn't easy working with so many different entities—county, state, and federal—and with forty or fifty people from a twelve-county area. Frankly, it was like herding cats. Our MPO director is a gentleman by the name of Michael Morris and I would say he has been magical in his ability to put together various pots of money and complete projects. Michael has been able to convince everyone to take off their individual hats when they walk into the room and to help the region, especially realizing that as our residents move from one area of the region to another, they don't see signs saying, "This road is now being maintained by somebody else." In the end, it is in our interest to set aside the preferences of one city or county and work in the best interest of all the citizens in our region.

Despite these gains, the biggest problem we're facing is maintaining the infrastructure we built. We haven't had a hike in our gas tax since the early 1990s, so that puts financial pressure on the Texas Department of Transportation. Likewise, as more electric vehicles come on the roads, the owners aren't paying anything for the use of the roads because they're not buying gas. Meanwhile, Texas as a whole is growing tremendously and traffic has grown, too. We still have oil and gas exploration and drilling. That means heavier trucks are on our local roads, and they can demolish those roads pretty quickly.

We not only need to repair the roads, we need to widen them. Yet one of the things that has prevented this is during the last three or four sessions of the state legislature, we have been prohibited from continuing our public-private partnerships. The legislature received some political pressure from citizen groups who objected to paying any toll on a Texas road. The problem is that without those tolls, we couldn't have built the road in the first place. So without the partnerships, we have lost a major tool in our toolbox to keep up with the congestion.

The North Tarrant Express is an example of how effective these partnerships have been. The state approved the project for a limited expansion. The price tag was close to a billion dollars. I spoke to the commissioner of the Texas Department of Transportation and he said TxDOT wanted to try a public-private partnership and see if they could persuade the private sector to help with the express project. The long and short of it turned out to be that the private sector came along. It became a $2.2 billion project. TxDOT put up $600 million. The developers came in with $1.6 billion. They basically rebuilt the existing road and added access lanes and four toll lanes, two in either direction, for a total of about fifteen miles. It turned out perfectly with the developers agreeing to handle the maintenance so we will be freed of that expense for the next half-century. When the road finally reverts back to the public, it can't be given back as rubble—it has to be in good condition.

The deal was beneficial to all concerned and I often tell residents that if we are going to keep people moving here, then we have to keep them moving after they get here. As long as we have this increasing population, building and maintaining this infrastructure will be a challenge. We have done a good job with respect to safety. We have our courtesy patrols out to help disabled vehicles get back on the road and when there's an accident, we get there quickly. In an effort to be able to control that, we've got signboards that talk about where the traffic is backed up or where there was an accident.

I have continued to push the legislature to rethink the public-private partnerships. However, there remains the political pressure not to move ahead. So many people thought we were bringing in outside investors, but that wasn't true. The most significant funding from the private sector came from the retirement funds of the Dallas fire and police departments, and it is paying an excellent return. I believe our bond projects have led to some very good roads within our different municipalities. We have helped connect communities and relieve some congestion in the downtown areas, making roads less dangerous. Over the past decade we have probably invested at least $10 billion on transportation projects within just Tarrant County. And it was probably the same for the decade before that. When you put all the money that the state, the feds, the private sector, the county, and the cities have put into these projects, we have easily allocated over $20 billion dollars in the last 20 years.

We are still not finished. In November 2021, we approved a $400 million next- generation transportation bond. We had a call for projects to partner with cities for up to $200 million. We have another $125 million that we will use for partnerships on multi-jurisdictional projects with the local, state, or federal government and another $75 million that we will utilize for various discretionary projects in Tarrant County. I recite all of this as a way to demonstrate the ongoing nature of dealing with roadways.

Right now, I'm afraid the public-private partnerships won't be coming back. I believe our state leadership is listening too much to the minority that may vote in the primary but will not vote in the same numbers in the general election. I think for the moment, that minority voice is having way too much of an impact on our state leaders.

I have been driving these roads for a long time. In fact, I can remember times when I didn't feel like there was much traffic at all driving from the northeast part of the county to downtown. Certainly now, depending upon the time of day that I go, it will take me longer to drive the thirteen miles to my office—say fifteen or twenty minutes— but it is still much better than the type of congestion that I've experienced when I've traveled to Austin or Houston or other major cities around the country. I still feel like it's because of the $20 billion we invested that we have almost kept pace with our population growth and tamped down our congestion level. We will have to push our roads program and other modal solutions over the next decade if we hope to continue to keep our congestion manageable.

AIRPORTS

Assistant County Manager Lorina Dellinger
Nye County, Nevada

"For those of us who choose to live amid the austere beauty in the isolated landscape of the desert, having access to airports and airplanes means peace of mind."

When people think of Nevada, they think of big casinos and the neon allure of the Las Vegas Strip. But that is not the reality in Nye County where I live and work. Nye County is dominated by vast desert lands crisscrossed by rugged mountains and steep valleys and dotted with vegetation that gave Nevada one of its nicknames, the Sagebrush State.

There are only 53,450 people in the entire county. By area, however, Nye County is the largest county in Nevada and the third-largest in the contiguous United States with a land mass of roughly 18,190 square miles. That's larger than Massachusetts, Connecticut, and Rhode Island combined. Given the difficult terrain and lack of population centers, the road and highway network in Nye County is rather limited. As a result, flying is on the rise.

It takes nearly six hours to drive from one end of Nye County to the other on U.S. 95, the only highway that traverses the county north to south. This lack of high-speed routes can spell disaster in an emergency. Getting medical help could be hours away driving across the barren landscape. This lifestyle is second-nature to me. I was raised in Tonopah and I've been a county employee for the past twenty years. It's somewhat of an understatement to say that I'm well-acquainted with the transportation challenges here.

Only about 3 percent of the county's land area is privately owned and the rest is predominantly public land managed by the federal and state government. That fact underscores our reliance on federal funding and the financial challenges and limitations for improving our transportation infrastructure. The reality is that we are dependent on the slow-motion procedures of Washington rather than the more rapid and nimble private sector.

KEY STATS

Counties are involved in the operation of 34 percent of public airports.

There are numerous factors behind a trend in increased aviation over ground transportation in Nye County. First of all, U.S. 95 has been described as one of the most dangerous highways in America because much of it is a two-lane highway and passing lanes are almost nonexistent. I actually have a friend from my school days who got her pilot's license so she didn't have to drive this highway. The accidents there are just unimaginable and driving while intoxicated is a growing problem. All of this adds up to a high rate of car crashes on these desolate stretches across the desert where cell phone reception is spotty at best and it may not be possible to summon emergency medical personnel.

These are some of the reasons why people with means are choosing to fly unencumbered across the county in a fraction of the time without the worry of traffic accidents or construction projects that further slow ground travel. Natural disasters can also impact ground transportation. A couple years ago, a major earthquake split apart a stretch of U.S. 95, disrupting our main artery for a lengthy period while repairs were made. Obviously, people with access to planes were not inconvenienced by the damage to the highway.

This increase in the use of privately owned planes and charter aircraft has cast an unflattering light on the challenges facing Nye County's airports. We have many deficiencies at our three rural airports: Tonopah, Beatty, and Gabbs. A lack of infrastructure is a major issue. For instance, the utilities in Tonopah and around the airport are owned and maintained by the town of Tonopah, not Nye County. The challenge of trying to expand our best and busiest airport, Tonopah, is that the town must approve all infrastructure improvements and development proposals, and that requires a lengthy, challenging approval process. The town and its engineers need to be consulted and must sign off on any new project, which also delays things and discourages developers.

Pahrump is the county's largest town with about 38,000 residents, located 60 miles west of Las Vegas. It has a private airport but not one for public use. We rely heavily and almost exclusively on the Federal Aviation Administration for grants to fund infrastructure improvements. For instance, we never had fuel tanks at the Beatty Airport before a recent installation, which has increased aircraft volume and also provides a critical medical transport link. The previous hospital in Tonopah closed five years ago, so a refueling stop in Beatty is a welcome development because county residents rely on medical flight services if critical care is required for any major trauma.

Another drawback is that the airports in Beatty and Gabbs do not have a fixed-base operator (FBO), meaning it is not staffed and is essentially a rural self-serve airstrip for pilots to get out and stretch their legs and use a bathroom. Also, Gabbs does not have a fueling station, which limits its usage. Even at Tonopah, our busiest airport which does have an FBO, it is only staffed part-time, although it does have a fueling station. Still, Tonopah is inadequate for the uptick in plane traffic, primarily recreational flights from Las Vegas and an increase in cargo carriers such as FedEx and UPS, which can cut hours off a route by air compared to driving on rural roads around large mountains. The FedEx and UPS express deliveries are a critical service for county businesses, who assign a staffer to drive to the airport to pick up important overnight packages.

Infrastructure improvements are difficult. A prime example of this is Gabbs, a mining community of about 100 people. The airport is essentially a dirt runway with minimal upkeep. We do send county workers to remove vegetation, fill in ditches, and grade humps and bumps. It is rarely used, for obvious reasons.

Looking to the future, we are at work on a master plan for the Tonopah Airport. We were fortunate that the acreage was deeded to Nye County by the federal government from land previously occupied by a U.S. Army airfield. We are hoping to create a renewable energy project on the open land outside the actual runway and airport operations. The challenge is that if a private developer wanted to build a warehouse, they would be a tenant of the federal government which owns the land, not the county. The land deed situation reduced the county's capital costs, but it makes it difficult to recruit private developers.

In terms of drafting a master plan for Nye County's airports to accommodate future needs and growth, the top priority is for emergency medical transport. Secondly, the number of private plane owners and charter operations is growing and time constraints and other drawbacks of driving on U.S. 95 have spurred a significant increase in aviation in the county.

When people ask me about the future of aviation in Nye County and my hopes for our three rural airports, I am optimistic. I believe we will continue to find ways to make improvements, including seeking more funding from the FAA and applying for grants from other sources as well. We have two large Army airfield hangars at Tonopah that we are hoping to renovate and repurpose. One thought floated by our facility director is to convert one to a hotel to meet the needs of pilots who are flying in from long distances and would welcome an opportunity to spend the night and rest up at Tonopah. We also would like to offer more services, such as a restaurant and a small market, so pilots would not have to call an Uber driver or a cab to take them into town several miles away.

Any future capital improvement plans will focus on renewable energy and sustainability, while also maintaining a key component of our airports, which is to provide emergency medical transport in order to support public safety and community healthcare through rapid aviation transportation to medical centers and hospitals in Nye County and beyond.

For those of us who choose to live amid the austere beauty in the isolated landscape of the desert, having access to airports and airplanes means peace of mind, knowing that acute care hospital services and emergency department specialists are just a short flight away.

TECHNOLOGY

BROADBAND

Judge/Executive Gary Moore
Boone County, Kentucky

"When I was elected, I never would have dreamed that we would have an opportunity to touch every home in Boone County with a technology that connects our residents to the world."

For some time, we knew our residents needed improved connections to the internet, but it was COVID-19 that proved how lacking the county was in coverage. Our schools purchased Chromebooks for the students, but at home, many of them couldn't connect to the web and parents had to search for public Wi-Fi so their children could do their schoolwork.

Prior to the pandemic, I was on a local hospital healthcare board, and we were trying to increase the number of e-healthcare visits. It was a struggle until COVID-19 came along, and e-visits were required. We went from doing just a few hundred of them a year to thousands within a couple months. That was the second indicator that high-speed connections were critical. And finally, there was the work-from-home component.

That was in the fall of 2020. At the time, I was the president of the National Association of Counties (NACo). Connectivity was a frequent topic of conversation, so I appointed a broadband task force. The members were from various parts of the country, from rural and urban areas, and from both sides of the political aisle. During the NACo task force meetings, every member expressed the same passion for broadband so when I got back home, I told my team—my county administrator and others—that we had to get something going quickly because with the pandemic in full swing, we might be facing a shortage of cable installers and fiber-optic cable.

KEY STATS

In rural areas, just 65 percent of residents have high-speed internet access via both fixed wireless services and mobile LTE broadband.

Prior to the pandemic, we had met with all our local telecoms, but no one had plans to expand broadband to every area. They were more concerned with the return on their investment than universal service. Once COVID-19 arrived, we knew there was going to be money coming from the federal government and hopefully from the state. In December, we wrote our request for quotes. Our goal was to identify the best strategic partner and then to negotiate all of the terms.

We began interviewing vendors. During those discussions, we discovered that there were a lot of different ways to tackle this problem. We heard about potential combinations of wireless and satellite products and other technologies, but we felt because of the size and nature of our county—mainly our hilly topography—that wireless wouldn't be as dependable as we'd like.

We chose fiber, which limited us to a handful of companies. Cincinnati Bell proposed a timeline that was much quicker than the others. The reason for that was—if you think back to landline telephones—Cincinnati Bell already had poles and old-style phone cabling and they had the ability to run the new high-speed fiber faster than their competitors. The negotiations over the completion timeline became interesting. They were thinking five to ten years for some of the outlying areas in our county and, in some areas that were more challenging, longer than ten years.

Our team felt that we needed the high-speed broadband now and we had to push hard on the schedule. They wanted more time to get this done, but I thought the longer counties wait, the tougher it was going to be because of the things I mentioned earlier—lack of contractors and cable.

By early 2021, Cincinnati Bell agreed to two years for installation, and that accounted for their selection as our vendor. Since then, they have been out running cable every day. After they run the cable, they have sales reps that follow those lines and knock on each door to make the resident aware that they are now connected.

Our plan offered something for everyone. What we found as the technology evolved was that frequently there would be fiber run to a node in a community, but from that node to the homes it would be collapsed copper, which didn't provide the same speed as fiber. But replacing that wire on an individual basis was cost prohibitive. One gentleman who had a home-based business needed high-speed broadband for his company. He had requested prices for extending fiber to his door and it was around $25,000. Understandably, he became an advocate for our plan. In addition to running in the rural areas of the county, we're also in suburban areas, and changing all of that cabling to the homes to fiber. When every home is done, we are going to upgrade multifamily units. That's a future year-long phase.

I was already a Cincinnati Bell Fioptics customer, but I had the old-style coaxial cable and the speed of the connection was spotty at times. I did not have the TiVo type box and options for the TV. With the new system, I do. Our personal need when we're home is more entertainment-related because most of us don't work from home full-time. However, a neighbor of mine works for the Internal Revenue Service out of her house and she is elated at the speed of the new system and how it is more dependable than what she had before. I don't know if her earlier connection was with Cincinnati Bell or one of their competitors. And the county does not have an exclusive contract with Cincinnati Bell. Any other company that wants to run cable or wireless is free to compete and operate in Boone County.

There have been some complaints from the community. It is more of a communication problem than a technological one. People are still skeptical that this is really happening. There was a customer or two who had the Cincinnati Bell product and claimed they weren't happy with it. That was the old technology, though, and we have been asking the community to let Cincinnati Bell prove that their technology is what they claim it to be. We're confident that those residents will have the same positive experience I had.

We have been keeping the community in the loop by several methods. Recently, we started a TextMyGov program. Residents can take a picture of a pothole and text it to us. Or they can ask us a question and we will text them the answer. We also post to our Facebook page, run televised commission meetings twice a month, and publish a county magazine, *What's Happening*, and mail it to every home. We did a big cover story on the cable rollout. Finally, there are the people who stop me in the grocery store, which is why elected officials go to the frozen food section last because it's not unusual to have a thirty-minute conversation before you can get to the checkout counter. These conversations are the essence of local government.

Naturally, financing of such a large project was a major concern. The initial price tag was $40 million. The county contributed $13.6 million. Cincinnati Bell was contractually committed to at least $30 million and would own the new infrastructure; our money was the taxpayers' contribution to capital outlay, not the operating of the system. I went to some other taxing agencies in the county—the school and library systems and the University of Kentucky. Together, they agreed to kick in a million dollars. My net amount was then $12.6 million. Our state legislature set aside funds from the American Rescue Plan Act to pay for broadband. The legislature has been a bit slow in answering our funding request, but they did set a $5 million cap that any county could get if we proved our need and that we were doing it properly. I have a $5 million request in to the Commonwealth of Kentucky Broadband Fund, which will further reduce the overall cost.

None of that money will cover the monthly bill for the users, though we negotiated the Boone County Affinity Package which provided discounted service. We also found that the Kentucky Department of Education offered help for students who were receiving a free or reduced lunch or any public assistance. They could get broadband at a sliding scale price and the lower the family income, the more the subsidy. Cincinnati Bell offers a program called UniCity and our contract calls for them to provide free public hotspots throughout the county. We are looking at the parks and other locations and we will continue to monitor the affordability question.

We believe our countywide technology will stimulate economic development. With so many companies not bringing everyone back to the office or instituting a hybrid arrangement and downsizing their commercial space, connecting homes is crucial to conducting business. We're one of the fastest-growing areas in the country and we have a workforce shortage. If we can connect people to jobs without requiring them to leave their homes, companies will have a whole new pool of potential employees.

Access to broadband has already improved medical services for county residents. The major healthcare system in Boone County is the Catholic diocesan-owned network of physicians, hospitals, and emergency departments. They have dramatically stepped up their ability to do e-health. I contracted COVID-19, the Omicron variant, even though I'd been vaccinated and boosted. My entire communication and coverage during that time was done online and it worked quite well.

In 1998 when I was elected, I never would have dreamed that we would have an opportunity to touch every home in Boone County with a technology that connects our residents to the world. But within a year, it will be true, and my team is proud of the role we played and of the impact this will have long after I've retired.

CYBERSECURITY

Director of Information Technology John Harrison
Franklin County, Virginia

"Negating apathy and adjusting long-standing cultures that see technology as a mysterious entity is part of my job as a leader in the technology space and public sector."

Most people don't give much thought to the vulnerability of their digital devices or the openings they give cybercriminals. We all routinely text friends and family on cellphones, communicate with colleagues through email from a PC or phone, shop online and bank on a laptop. We relax with our favorite episodes on our tablets and tell Alexa what music to play.

Sometimes, we might remember to set up strong passwords resistant to a cyberattack, but probably not. Somehow things just seem to work, until they don't, and a malware attack has frozen the computer, your work data is being held hostage by ransomware saboteurs, or a hacker has cleaned out your bank account. That's where the hard-working "good guys" come in. I've spent over two decades in the private and public sectors and as a director of IT, it is my job to keep my county's computer systems, digital networks, and online applications secure and fully operational while making the technology as user friendly and supportive of business goals as possible. We provide technology solutions to enable the business of local government to be effective and to respond to the needs of our residents.

Over my career, the frequency, sophistication, and intensity of cyberattacks has grown exponentially, which puts constant pressure on limited resources and staff. Numerous areas of need constantly compete for funding even though we focus on driving down costs and expenditures. Additionally, showing the benefit of funding cyber-related technology is a risk-based discussion and difficult to express. People can conceptually understand physical security, like protecting a bank. It is far more difficult to visualize the security requirements to safeguard digital data.

KEY STATS

Only 30 percent of counties have implemented a .gov domain.

That causes problems in explaining vulnerability because most people view the world as a physical construct. But cyberspace isn't physical, it's digital, and in the digital world the guy trying to break into the bank doesn't live down the street. He could be anywhere and could be acting alone, as part of a group, or at the behest of a nation-state. He doesn't necessarily know, or care, who I am. I'm just a digital entity and a potential payoff.

He simultaneously attacks me and any number of others in a variety of ways. It could be through phishing or cross-site scripting. Whatever the case, he's deploying a large number of attacks to a large number of targets. Suppose my neighbor avoids a phishing attack, and I use that to showcase the possibility of such an attack impacting my own organization. The response would very likely be, "Aren't you glad you sent out the phishing warning last month so everybody knew not to click on that link?"

I would be glad, but unless you cover every potentiality, you haven't closed all the doors. A breach can occur without you knowing about it until another entity—the FBI, for example—contacts you and says, "We just found your entire active directory for sale on the dark web." That happens more often than we would like to admit, usually because most organizations simply cannot afford or staff against the barrage of attacks and also maintain their primary business function. That is especially true in public service. This means they don't necessarily have the latest and greatest tools to monitor and prevent those types of activities or the trained staffing levels to meet the rising tide of attacks. Funding and staffing are primarily for the immediate citizen service-related needs like 911, law enforcement, emergency response, or social services. In nearly every local government, the needs quickly outstrip the funding sources.

IT department budgets receive roughly the same allocation year after year. This is because technology is something few take the time to understand. The result is that the technologists have approximately the same resources in 2022 that they had over the past decade—despite the growing number of successful attacks in the public sector. I routinely look for cost savings and renegotiate contracts to find funds to cover those increasing needs and security costs. The ability to do this is limited.

Another pressing issue is the difficulty of finding qualified IT staff. As our employees retire or leave for higher-paying private-sector jobs, it is harder to recruit staff to replace them at a price the local tax base can support. Long-term employees have grown accustomed to the salary range along with the cost-of-living adjustments that seldom match inflation. Those young or new to the workforce are looking for job flexibility and salaries that immediately compensate or compete against current interest rates and costs. Take my locality as an example. Franklin County, Virginia, is a largely rural county in the Blue Ridge foothills with a population of 55,000. It is a lovely place to live and raise a family and while it offers many opportunities, I wouldn't classify it as a hot spot for technology. We are blessed to have the staff we do, but recruiting and retaining in-demand technologists is difficult. Local government is growing more accustomed to job postings that do not receive a single resume.

Most small and medium-sized localities like ours cannot afford to hire specialized cybersecurity engineers and to keep them trained because they are in high demand. We hire other positions at a salary easier to absorb and attempt to have cybersecurity tasks performed by staff that lack the skillsets in that area. Meanwhile, the overall skill level required for our IT department to succeed continues to rise with initiatives like interactive web content, chatbots, Internet of Things, high-speed broadband to rural areas to close the digital divide, or next-generation 911 emergency-call systems. Local government leaders want the best for their communities, and the citizens deserve it. The limiting factor is the balance of service delivery versus the willingness of residents and businesses to support those services with higher taxes.

With respect to technology, that relationship is further undermined by not understanding the risks posed by a digital world. Likewise, a staffing shortage puts in motion what could be described as the outsource trap. Since I don't have the internal staffing or time required for the large, time-sensitive projects, I am forced to outsource that work, in part or in total depending on the scope and complexity of the project. The trap is an insidious one and occurs over time when internal staff are isolated from the technologies that others have helped implement.

Internal resources eventually lack the know-how to maintain the new systems and infrastructure because they did not install it and were not trained on it. In many cases, there is no time or funding allocated to maintain their training. When that happens, we can't blame staff because the funding was not available to maintain their level of training.

I feel strongly that the technology industry in general, but the public sector specifically, needs to overhaul and upgrade the funding models in order to keep up with citizen needs and future IT projects. We are losing the leverage of excellent retirement benefits, which had been a strong benefit to recruit IT experts to government work. That advantage has been somewhat countered by tech companies who have improved their benefit packages or whose pay scale outpaces the local government's retirement contribution. On the public-facing side of my job, the challenge is to develop awareness around matters of cybersecurity and to educate county employees, local government personnel, and residents about the clear and present danger—and financial burdens—of malicious cyberattacks or ransomware strikes.

Negating apathy and adjusting long-standing cultures that see technology as a mysterious entity is part of my job as a leader in the technology space and public sector. Cybersecurity is not solely a technology problem. It is an issue that, at its core, is more related to human behavior and perception. We build habits to stay safe as we go through our daily lives, but we push back on developing habits digitally. Why? Because technology remains something that should just work, without individual understanding. That divide is what I and every technology leader try to address. No technology will solve or close human behavioral gaps. Address the perception, adjust the behavior, and cybersecurity can mature into a supportive safeguard of our personal lives and a pillar to organizational health.

CLERKS/RECORDERS

Recorder Chad Airhart
Dallas County, Iowa

"We do play a small and important part in helping the residents of our county and state to live the lives they want to live."

I'm a seventh-generation Iowan and in college I majored in history, so I appreciate the records in our office beyond their legal utility. Yes, it's important for the protection of buyers and sellers that we have real-estate transactions on file. Yet Iowa became a state in 1846, and we've had recorder's offices in all of our counties since then. Those old documents—the deeds; marriage certificates; birth, death, and military-service records—tell the story of how county residents lived and died. They are our heritage. I understand the legal reason for records, but I never lose sight of their historical meaning.

Dallas County is the fourth-fastest growing county in America, and it has been in the top ten almost continuously for the last eighteen years. I came into office in 2011, and that first year we recorded 18,551 documents. A decade later it was 37,715 documents and we had fewer staff than when I started. While we were dealing with the increased workload, we also tackled the project of looking at our records and deciding how to modernize our approach to storing them.

We had two separate software systems, an arrangement that, to put it mildly, was less than ideal. One software system was for indexing, the other for imaging, and we had to marry them together. It wasn't working and I thought, "Here we are, a rapidly growing county with one of the highest median incomes in the United States and we're not utilizing the most efficient tools."

KEY STATS

There are 3.6 million county employees as of 2022.

Our top priority was to image and index our military records so they were retrievable in the event that veterans required a copy to receive their benefits. We were anxious to complete this as soon as possible to protect the records from a fire or tornado or any other disaster. This was our first step to see how the project worked. When we were done, we decided to digitize everything and put it online for the public to access. Some of the smaller record books had legal-sized paper in them, and our staff began to image as many of those as we could. We had to disassemble the bigger books to scan those pages. Our old software was making this process difficult and we searched high and low for a new package.

Finally, we found Resolution3 by Cott Systems. That find was the reason why we were able to do twice as much work with essentially the same number of staff. The only records we couldn't handle were in the big, old books that didn't come apart; they were sewn and bound just like a book you would buy at Barnes & Noble. We asked Cott to take care of that scanning. They brought in a scanner the size of two washing machines put together and scanned those books one page at a time.

It has been approximately five years since we launched the software. My original goal was to image and index our records to 1970. We managed to get to the early 1960s and even scan some things from the 1950s. We didn't feel a need to go further back. More important is that with the Cott software, we have records up online. Now, the banker, the abstract company, or the real estate lawyer trying to find a document can find it on the search page of our website with a few keystrokes. They no longer have to drive to the county courthouse, park, go through security, come to our office, locate the record, pay for a photocopy, and then drive back home.

It has made the recording of new documents far easier. Now, when someone comes in with a document or one arrives in the mail, we record it with the same software we use for our daily accounting. It's all in one system so when we receive payment, it prints the receipt, and the data we just typed into the computer is already online. Then we scan the document and five minutes later it is online. Right after we switched to this system, a lot of people told us they wished every county operated the same way. That felt good to get that kind of affirmation and in general, I always feel that I was able to help government work for the public.

With the dramatic increase in our county population and the officials and paperwork that come with it, space for government offices is at a premium. The courthouse isn't getting any bigger, but the court's demands are expanding and administrative offices kept moving out until there were only two left in the courthouse—the recorder and the treasurer. Our office is about a third of the square footage it was when I arrived in 2011. That's because our real-estate record books are no longer here. We store them in an archives area. I believe we are the only recorder's office in Iowa that doesn't have to share space with their real-estate books.

With our records stored digitally in the cloud and backed up in multiple storage facilities, we have a hedge against disaster. If somehow the courthouse vanished along with our records, all we would have to do is turn on a laptop and find an internet connection and we would have a fully functioning recorder's office.

It has always been my mantra that we should be a self-sustaining operation. The way our budget works is that we cover all the expenses associated with our office. I pay for our share of the janitor's crew, the light and heat bills, and our office supplies. We fund our whole payroll, our share of workers compensation insurance, and pay into their retirement. The state sets our fees and we collect them. Despite our overhead, we bring in more money over the counter than we spend. For the twelve fiscal years that I've been a part of the recorder's office, we have returned a fund balance to the county's general fund of $4,237,000, which helps to reduce property taxes. We have accomplished that while modernizing the office and doubling our workload. This fiscal year we're on track to return $1 million to the county.

I can envision a time that's not too far away when paper records belong to the past. For example, right now we have a statewide electronic recording system, Iowa Land Records. It's a portal so, for instance, if a bank in Denver is financing a property sale, the papers can be signed in the bank and filed here through the portal. In addition, as the imaging of records becomes more common and local governments understand the cost savings associated with less office space and how easy it is to access and store electronic records, paper will slowly disappear.

In short, electronic records enable governments to work more efficiently for their constituents. Daily, for me, when I help somebody because he needs to find a copy of his second wife's marriage certificate from 1970 so they can get Social Security figured out, or when I help someone retrieve a death certificate so they can collect life insurance, or when I get birth certificates for a couple so they can apply for passports to travel somewhere they have always wanted to go. I have an enormous sense of satisfaction. True, we are simply an administrative office of government, but we do play a small and important part in helping the residents of our county and state to live the lives they want to live.

APPENDIX

*A written statement for the record by National Association of Counties
CEO/Executive Director Matthew D. Chase who testified before the House
of Representatives Subcommittee on Government Operations Committee on
Oversight and Reform on July 23, 2019.*

Chairman Connolly, Ranking Member Meadows and members of the
Subcommittee, thank you for the opportunity to testify on "Restoring
the Partnership: The Future of Federalism in America."

My name is Matthew Chase and I serve as the CEO/Executive
Director of the National Association of Counties (NACo). Founded
in 1935, NACo is the only national association representing America's
3,069 counties, parishes and boroughs, including nearly 40,000 county
elected officials and more than 3.6 million county employees. The
association advocates for county priorities in federal policy making,
promotes exemplary county policies and practices, nurtures leadership
and knowledge networks, optimizes county and taxpayer resources,
and enriches the public's understanding of county government. NACo's
ultimate purpose is to build healthy, safe, and vibrant counties across
the nation.

NACo is also a member of the Big 7 coalition in Washington,
D.C., which is comprised of the national associations representing state
and local elected officials. This coalition includes NACo, along with
the National Governors Association, National League of Cities, U.S.
Conference of Mayors, the Council of State Governments, National
Conference of State Legislatures and the International City/County
Management Association.

Today, Mr. Chairman, I would like to share three main points
about our nation's current form of federalism and our ideas for

strengthening the intergovernmental partnership of federal, state, local, and tribal officials. This includes our overall support for creating a new, modern, national forum for advancing and facilitating improved intergovernmental relations.

1. Counties play an important, fundamental role in our intergovernmental system with significant policy, service delivery, and administrative roles and responsibilities
2. Early, consistent, and meaningful engagement with intergovernmental partners is vital in the development and implementation of effective policies, programs, and regulations, even when competing visions and priorities might exist throughout levels of government, and
3. The establishment of a new national commission on intergovernmental relations would help create a better system of federalism that benefits all levels of government and, most importantly, the public we serve.

Public trust in institutions, including government, is at an all-time low, and dysfunction and a lack of coordination and dialogue between levels of government are key contributors to this trend. Our Founding Fathers established a brilliant form of federalism with multiple layers of checks and balances, including across the three federal branches and between the federal government and state governments. One of our main lessons learned in modern times is that while there is a clear distinction and separation of powers and duties among these levels of government, there is also a deep interconnectedness and interdependence. This bond is a shared purpose to achieve public policy outcomes that serve the American public, often requiring the collective efforts of federal, state, local and tribal governments working together.

In recent decades, we have witnessed a significant decline in a structured, intentional dialogue and partnership between federal, state, and local government officials. While we recognize deep political divides, competing partisan visions, and a lack of political incentives for partnerships and compromise in today's climate, the vast challenges facing the nation require a new pathway for intergovernmental relations, including with the private, nonprofit, philanthropic, and academic sectors.

Our nation, states, counties, and other localities are highly diverse and vary immensely in social and political systems, as well as cultural, economic, and structural circumstances. In our case, despite this diversity, all counties fulfill many similar mandates and duties. We are responsible for supporting and maintaining public infrastructure, transportation and economic development assets, providing justice, law enforcement and public safety services, and protecting the public's health and well-being.

While some of these responsibilities are unique to counties, in many cases we work with our state and federal partners to achieve optimal solutions. These responsibilities are the shared, fundamental components of a broader national interest in serving our citizens. Policies and programs established by the federal government are intended to guide and coordinate efforts, but are ultimately implemented at the state and local levels. That is why federal policies matter to states, counties, and cities, and why states and local governments matter to federal policies.

NACo and our state and local partners support the formation of a national commission to facilitate intergovernmental cooperation, based on the lessons learned of the Advisory Commission on Intergovernmental Relations (ACIR) and other previous national efforts. With emerging issues such as cybersecurity, artificial intelligence, and advanced automation, we need a neutral forum for elected policymakers from all levels of government to focus on a shared purpose, including balancing the scale of federal powers and resources with the rights, responsibilities, capabilities, and innovations of states, local governments, and tribal officials.

County Role in the Intergovernmental System

First, Mr. Chairman, counties play an important, fundamental role in our intergovernmental system with significant policy, service delivery, and administrative roles and responsibilities. County governments affect the lives of Americans across the country every day and provide vital services, including those mandated by federal and state policies, as well as those requested by local residents. America's 3,069 counties:

- Build and maintain the largest share of public road miles (46 percent); own four out of every ten bridges; and support one-third of airports and nearly 80 percent of public transportation systems
- Support nearly 1,000 safety net hospitals, 1,900 public health departments, 750 behavioral health authorities, and 900 skilled nursing facilities
- Operate nine out of every 10 local jails with nearly 12 million inmates each year
- Fund and manage over 100,000 polling places for federal, state, and local elections
- Invest in human services such as senior and child protective services, workforce skills training, early childhood development, and veterans' programs
- Manage a wide range of public facilitates, such as libraries, community centers, parks, museums, and ports
- Invest in sewage and solid waste disposal, recycling, and environmental stewardship, and
- Maintain vital records, such as birth certificates, marriage licenses, court documents, and land records.

Counties are incredibly diverse with respect to population and geography, ranging in area from 26 square miles (Arlington County, Va.) to 87,860 square miles (North Slope Borough, Alaska). The population of counties varies from Loving County, Texas, with 112 residents, to

Los Angeles County, Calif., which is home to 10.2 million people and would be the eighth largest state on its own. Only 40 counties have over one million residents, while 2,120 (or 70 percent of) counties have populations under 50,000. In fact, half of the U.S. population resides in just 144 large urban counties, while roughly 2,900 counties are home to the other 50 percent of the U.S. population.

All told, counties across the country serve nearly 310 million residents, employ 3.6 million people and invest nearly $600 billion annually in local programs and services, including those mandated by federal and state directives. Counties also service vast areas of federal public land, with 63 percent of counties having federal public land within their boundaries. Counties matter to America, and therefore, federal policies matter to counties.

Counties play an often-misunderstood role in our intergovernmental system, with a unique position to understand the diverse needs of our local communities. State and local governments' experience and expertise can help identify creative, cost-effective methods to address issues and can better identify and mitigate potential impacts to localities that may be overlooked without continuous, engaged intergovernmental cooperation.

Current Intergovernmental Relations Hold Both Tension and Promise

Second, Mr. Chairman, early, consistent, and meaningful engagement with intergovernmental partners is vital in the development and implementation of effective policies, programs and regulations, even when competing visions and priorities exist throughout levels of government. Today's complex public policy issues—both challenges and opportunities—are often interrelated and cross multiple federal, state, and local jurisdictions and responsibilities.

There are few federal and state programs that do not interact with counties in some manner. The complexity of issues facing federal, state and local governments necessitate a strong and institutionalized national forum for intergovernmental collaboration in order to produce optimal results for our residents. To better underscore this complexity, I would like to highlight four policy areas that impact all levels of government and our shared constituents:

1. **The Opioid Crisis.** Substance use and abuse, often with co-occurring mental health issues, has touched every corner of our country over the past few years. Counties have felt the impacts acutely. As individuals and their families experience an overdose, for example, just think about the number of potential contacts with our county services: dispatch calls typically go through county 911 and sheriffs' offices, individuals are often transported to county hospitals and jails, children are managed by county child welfare caseworkers, states and counties pay for prosecutors, public defenders, jail health care professionals, and investigators, and in the worst-case scenarios, county coroners are responsible for examining overdose deaths in overflowing county morgues. We are greatly appreciative of recent bipartisan federal efforts by Congress and the White House to assist us with this devastating and evolving crisis, but we still have major challenges ahead as a nation.

2. **Disasters and Emergency Management.** Local government officials are the first responders to natural disasters and other major emergencies. Without proper federal and state assistance, recovery and mitigation efforts may lack the full capabilities and resources necessary to be successful. In the past two years, more than 830 counties (25 percent of all counties) received a presidential disaster declaration, and in 2018 alone the federal government provided more than $130 billion for disaster relief and mitigation. However, this funding is routed through dozens of different programs with varying mandates, timelines, application procedures, and other complications states and local governments must navigate during dire times

of need. We understand that this level of federal investment is not sustainable. There is an immediate need for public sector partners, in cooperation with the private and nonprofit sectors, to develop a more sustainable national strategy for community resilience and disaster mitigation.

3. **Election Security.** Although the federal government, states, counties, and other local jurisdictions have different roles in our election process, we must all work together to ensure the integrity and security of our election systems. In any given election, we are only as secure as our weakest link: a failure in the chain at any point could cause major problems in the rest of the system. In 2018, Congress authorized $380 million for election security improvements; however, much of this funding was directed and held at the state level rather than reaching the county and local levels where we play a significant, direct role in purchasing and maintaining election equipment and operating polling locations. The Help America Vote Act (HAVA), which was implemented in 2002, improved intergovernmental coordination and systems upgrades, though the momentum was short-lived. As Congress continues to consider legislation that will directly impact state and local election administrators, a robust consultation process would strengthen the integrity, efficiency, and quality of our election systems.

4. **Public Lands.** Both the Federal Land Policy Management Act (FLPMA) and the National Forest Management Act are clear that the U.S. Department of the Interior (DOI) and the U.S. Forest Service are to coordinate their land management plans with localities, giving counties a voice in the process. Federal land management plans determine how a national forest is managed, where the public can recreate on federal lands, wildlife habitat conservation and resource extraction. These decisions impact watersheds, economic opportunity, public health, and county governments' revenue streams. However, federal agencies have met these mandates unevenly, leading to conflict with

local governments. While the current White House has worked to improve coordination of land use planning, more controls must be put in place. This would ensure the federal government upholds its end of the bargain and utilizes expertise county governments can offer. Enhanced coordination would help to make federal land management plans consistent with local needs, while also meeting our responsibilities as good stewards of our nation's resources and the environment.

The list of issues that demand a more modern, practical approach from the public sector is lengthy, from examining and preparing for the impacts of artificial intelligence to updating tax systems to preparing future generations of our workforce and our aging population. We are even launching a new partnership with the U.S. Department of Defense to better understand how local land use decisions and development patterns, such as housing, renewable energy, and conservation projects, impact our nation's military readiness.

In each of these examples, the roles and responsibilities of county governments evolve as local conditions and needs change with shifting economies, demographics, and overburdened infrastructure. However, our ability to adapt is constrained by federal and state mandates, and often any mandates passed from the federal government to states are then passed to local governments. Forty-five states also place limitations on county property tax authority, and the number of restrictions has expanded significantly since the 1990s. Only 29 states authorize counties to collect sales taxes, but almost always under various restrictions: twenty-six impose a sales tax limit and 19 require voter approval.

At the same time, NACo interviews reveal nearly three-quarters (73 percent) of states have escalated the number and/or cost of mandates for counties over the past decade, decreased state funding to counties over the past decade, or imposed a combination of both. Meanwhile, federal changes such as capping the state and local tax (SALT) deduction and eliminating advance refunding bonds have constrained fiscal options for both states and local governments.

In an environment where cities and counties have truncated financial flexibility, a strong intergovernmental partnership is even more important to ensure available dollars and resources are deployed effectively. To that end, we urge Congress to pass the Restore the Partnership Act and join states, counties, tribal governments, and other localities in supporting our system of federalism to the fullest extent possible.

Congress Should Establish a National Commission on Intergovernmental Relations

Finally, Mr. Chairman, the establishment of a new national commission on intergovernmental relations would help create a better system of federalism that benefits all levels of government and, most importantly, the public we serve. While we recognize that there appears to be very little political reward or incentive for this concept, history shows that our nation is strongest when we envision and pursue public policy goals together in a sustainable, practical way for all Americans, across all levels of government.

Counties – along with our other state and local association partners – urge Congress to embrace this commitment to intergovernmental participation. The bipartisan Restore the Partnership Act from Reps. Gerry Connolly (D-Va.) and Rob Bishop (R-Utah) takes an important step towards this commitment by establishing a national Commission on Intergovernmental Relations. We can respect and protect the unique roles and responsibilities of each level of government (and our non-governmental partners), while also creating new forums that help us pursue joint actions that are collaborative, performance driven and leverage our combined investments and assets.

Currently, the federal relationship with states and local governments varies greatly among branches of the federal government and among agencies within the federal government. When legislation is introduced, the Unfunded Mandates Reform Act (UMRA) ensures that a bill does not include an unreasonable unfunded mandate on state and local governments, at least to a certain extent. In recent years, Congress has found new ways to circumvent these restrictions, including adding in new grant conditions, increasing matching requirements or punting specific decisions to federal agencies. While we have pursued updates to UMRA, the current law still provides some protection for the federalism process in any new legislation.

Federal agencies, however, do not operate consistent intergovernmental processes. While Executive Order 13132 nominally requires agencies to engage in a federalism consultation process, this is adhered to unevenly not only across agencies, but often within a specific agency or regions of a specific agency. For example, the U.S. Department of Transportation may consider "early in the process" to mean during the public comment period, while the U.S. Environmental Protection Agency may interpret it to mean before a draft rule is released to the public. Similarly, for rules determined on a regional basis within a department or agency, each region may have a different process for engaging other governmental stakeholders.

These discrepancies make it difficult for states and local governments, including our national associations, to navigate the federalism process. This is concerning because the best solutions – those that meet the needs of our residents and are practically applicable on the ground – are most often developed in concert with all governmental stakeholders. This is not a political issue. Rather, we hope that by supporting the Restore the Partnership Act and forming this new Commission, Congress will affirm the federal government's seat at the table with its intergovernmental partners.

As outlined by former ACIR official Bruce McDowell in an April 2011 article, in the 1990s, the ACIR served a valuable role by "interjecting intergovernmental principles into the dialogue" at the federal level. For over three decades, the ACIR championed the idea that America's federal, state, and local governments need to work together if they are to serve the nation's citizens well." In addition, McDowell noted that governments "work best when they work together, each providing what it does best in a balanced partnership with the others."

Following the disbanding of the ACIR, the strong partnership between governments faded and local and state governments have faced increased mandates and a loss of local control from our federal counterparts. Intergovernmental collaboration requires bipartisan—and even nonpartisan—commitment to pursuing the best means of serving our constituents. Forming a new Commission on Intergovernmental Relations would inject a much-needed sense of governmental cooperation into our policy making process.

In addition to clarifying the regulatory process, states and local governments urge Congress to include its intergovernmental partners early and often in the legislative process. States and local governments, and our national associations, serve as a repository for policy ideas ripe for federal partnership. This includes direct interaction with state and local elected officials. The Big 7 coalition and our other state and local elected official associations are governmental partners, often representing the same taxpayers and residents. We are not a collection of special interest groups, and we share public accountability with our federal counterparts.

With today's increasingly complex public policy issues, we now need a neutral forum for elected policymakers from all levels of government to focus on a shared purpose, including balancing the scale of federal powers and resources with the rights, responsibilities, capabilities and innovations of states, local governments and tribal officials. It is important that we acknowledge the interconnectedness of the public sector and recommit to elevating our dialogue and professional relationships. As our Founding Fathers demonstrated, we can have intense, rigorous debates and viewpoints, while still embracing a boundary-crossing institution that can facilitate intergovernmental relations and effective intergovernmental partnerships.

Conclusion

Chairman Connolly, Ranking Member Meadows and members of the Subcommittee, thank you again for your leadership on this matter and for bringing the county voice to the table to discuss the importance of a robust federal, state, local, and tribal partnership. County officials stand ready with innovative approaches and solutions to work side by side with our federal and state partners to ensure the health, well-being, and safety of our citizens.

ACKNOWLEDGMENT

Thank you to all thirty county leaders who shared their stories of public service. Without their willingness to participate, this book would not be possible.

Many thanks to Chad Airhart, Mary Ann Borgeson, Joel Bousman, Stuart Clason, Lisa Cloninger, Lorina Dellinger, James Gore, John Harrison, Ricky Hatch, Amanda Heidecker, Lisa Janicki, Larry Johnson, Jennifer Llewellyn, David Montgomery, Gary Moore, Cathrene Nichols, Nancy O'Malley, Dotti Owens, Toni Preckwinkle, Connie Rockco, Manuel "Manny" Ruiz, Luis Sanchez, Janet Thompson, Pamela Tokar-Ickes, Nora Vargas, Dakisha (DK) Wesley, Robert Weygandt, Glen Whitley, Denise Winfrey, and Derek Young.

With gratitude to the NACo Executive Committee and Board of Directors for sharing the vision and dedicating resources to support this book.

Thank you to Rachel Looker, Mary Ann Barton, Charlie Ban, Hugh Clarke, Meredith Moran, Leon Lawrence III, Stephenie Overman, Dakota Hendricks, Matthew Chase, Brian Namey and Mark LaVigne for all their hard work every step of the way.

ABOUT THE AUTHOR

Peter Golden is an award-winning journalist, historian, novelist, and the author of nine books. He has interviewed Presidents Nixon, Ford, Reagan, and Bush (41); Secretaries of State Kissinger, Haig, and Shultz; Israeli Prime Ministers Rabin, Peres, and Shamir; and Soviet President Gorbachev. His latest novel, *Nothing Is Forgotten*, which explores the connection between the Holocaust and the Cold War, is published by Atria Books/Simon & Schuster. He lives outside Albany, New York.

CPSIA information can be obtained
at www.ICGtesting.com
Printed in the USA
LVHW032053030223
738624LV00013B/16/J

9 781665 736374